Recursion via Pascal

D0061199

Also in this series

19 Cambridge Computer Science Texts

Recursion via Pascal

J. S. Rohl

University of Western Australia

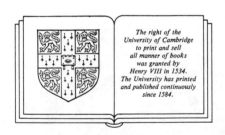

The right of the
University of Cambridge
to print and sell
all manner of books
was granted by
Henry VIII in 1534.
The University has printed
and published continuously
since 1584.

Cambridge University Press

Cambridge

London New York New Rochelle

Melbourne Sydney

Published by the Press Syndicate of the University of Cambridge
The Pitt Building, Trumpington Street, Cambridge CB2 1RP
32 East 57th Street, New York, NY 10022, USA
10 Stamford Road, Oakleigh, Melbourne 3166, Australia

© Cambridge University Press 1984

First published 1984
Reprinted 1986

Printed in Great Britain at the University Press, Cambridge

Library of Congress catalogue card number: 83-26335

British Library cataloguing in publication data
Rohl, J. S.
Recursion via Pascal. – (Cambridge computer science texts; 19)
1. Electronic digital computers – programming
2. Recursive functions
I. Title
001.64′2   QA76.6

ISBN 0 521 26329 8 hard covers
ISBN 0 521 26934 2 paperback

DJ

Contents

Preface

Recursion is the cinderella of programming techniques where languages such as Pascal are concerned. All primers mention it, of course, but generally devote only a few pages to it. Rohl and Barrett's *Programming via Pascal* is one of the more generous: it contains one chapter of 12 pages on the subject!

Books appropriate to second courses in programming, such as those by Wirth (1976), Alagic & Arbib (1978), and the more modern data structures texts, have helped considerably; but currently there is no book devoted to the use of recursion in Pascal or similar languages.

And yet this used not to be the case: Barron's delightful little book *Recursive Techniques in Programming* was published in 1968! Sadly it is now out of print, and in any event was beginning to show its age. *Recursion via Pascal* is the author's attempt to fill this gap.

Of course, in functional programming, recursion has received its full due, since it is quite often the only repetitive construct, and this area is fairly well served with text-books. In *Recursion via Pascal*, most of the examples are procedures rather than functions, partly because that is the usual Pascal style and partly because we want to give examples which actually do something, like drawing the cover motif of this series, instead of merely having a value. Reading one of the functional texts after finishing this book would provide an alternative perspective.

The material could have been organised in a number of ways. I have chosen to present it in what seems to me to be in order of increasing complexity. Generally the chapters come in pairs, one which considers data structures and one which does not. Chapters 1 and 2 introduce linear recursion, which arises in a procedure which calls itself only once. When a procedure calls itself twice we have binary recursion, which is considered in Chapters 3 and 4. Chapter 5 is an interlude in which we consider special situations such as mutual recursion and recursive calls. *N*-ary recursion, where a procedure calls itself a number of times, is treated in Chapters 6 and 7. Finally in Chapter 8 we consider how recursion may be eliminated.

Many helpful suggestions about the presentation of the material were made by Cambridge University Press's reviewers, David Barron and Chris Hawksley, to whom my thanks are due.

A first draft of much of this book was written while on sabbatical leave at the University of Edinburgh, and I am grateful to Sidney Michaelson and Peter Schofield for their hospitality, and to Dorothy McKie and Gina Temple who typed those drafts.

The final drafts were prepared by Joyce Fisher, and all the programs were tested and corrected by Janet Brockman. My special thanks to these two.

Perth, July 1983   J.S. Rohl

1
Introduction to recursion

What is recursion? It is simply a technique of describing something partly in terms of itself. This notion has wide applicability. We are all used to the idea that an adjectival clause, for example, may contain another adjectival clause. Who has not at sometime or another recited *This is the house that Jack built*?

> This is the cock that crowed in the morn
> That woke the priest all shaven and shorn
> That married the man all tattered and torn
> That kissed the maiden all forlorn
> That milked the cow with the crumpled horn
> That tossed the dog
> That worried the cat
> That killed the rat
> That ate the malt
> That lay in the house that Jack built.

On a more prosaic level, if you were asked for the differential with respect to x of $x^2 + 5x$ you would instantly, and correctly, reply $2x + 5$. If you were pressed to explain your answer you would probably reply, firstly, that the differential of $x^2 + 5x$ is equal to the differential of x^2 plus the differential of $5x$, and, secondly, that the differential of x^2 is $2x$ and of $5x$ is 5. This then is the essence of recursion which consists of two parts:

(i) the *recursive rule*: $\dfrac{d}{dx}(x^2 + 5x) = \dfrac{d}{dx}(x^2) + \dfrac{d}{dx}(5x)$

in which the differential of a sum is defined in terms of the differential of the two terms;

(ii) the *explicitly defined cases*: $\dfrac{d}{dx}(x^2) = 2x, \quad \dfrac{d}{dx}(5x) = 5$

which terminate the recursion.

For more general expressions, of course, we need further recursive rules, such as those for products and quotients, and more explicitly defined cases, such as that for the differential of a constant. We will return to this example in Chapter 3.

What are the advantages of recursion as a programming technique? From the point of view of this monograph there are four.

(i) For many problems the recursive solution is more natural than the alternative non-recursive solution. Of course naturalness is in the eye of the beholder and for some readers an unfamiliarity with recursion may indeed make the early examples appear unnatural. However the relationship between recursively defined data structures and recursive procedures is very close and by the time trees are introduced in Chapter 3 the appropriateness of recursion will be clear enough.

(ii) It is often relatively easy to prove the correctness of recursive procedures. Inasmuch as recursive procedures are direct transliterations of the mathematical formulations involved, the proofs are often trivial. Even where they are not, the proofs are based on the very familiar process of induction.

(iii) Recursive procedures are relatively easy to analyse to determine their performance. The analysis produces recurrence relations, many of which can easily be solved.

(iv) Recursive procedures are flexible. This is a very subjective statement but, as we demonstrate in Chapter 7 and elsewhere, it is quite easy to convert a general procedure into a more specific one. Indeed this is often a useful design technique: first write a program for a problem which is a generalisation of the given problem, and then adapt it to the problem in hand.

What are the costs to be incurred in using recursion? There are two:

(i) Recursive procedures may run more slowly than the equivalent non-recursive ones. There are two causes for this. Firstly, a compiler may implement recursive calls badly. Most, if not all, Pascal compilers handle recursion quite well and so the cost is small, perhaps 5% to 10%, perhaps nothing. At worst, as we shall shortly show, a recursive procedure may run at half-speed though this applies only to the most trivial procedures. Secondly, the recursive procedures we write may simply be inefficient. It is easy to write such procedures as we shall see, and we must always be on our guard to avoid doing so.

(ii) Recursive procedures require more store than their non-recursive counterparts. Each recursive call involves the creation of an activation record, and if the depth of recursion is large this space

2

penalty may be significant. This only arises with simple procedures, however: with more complex procedures the depth is small, and, what is more, the non-recursive versions themselves require space which is proportional to the recursive depth. Furthermore, there are some situations where the cost of the recursion, in both time and space, can be eliminated quite simply by a compiler.

With this in mind we now consider some simple examples all of which exhibit *linear recursion*. In these procedures there is only one recursive call. Others, such as the differentiation procedure referred to above, have two recursive calls, and we refer to this as *binary recursion*. Yet others have an indefinite number (the one written call is within a loop), and we refer to this as *n-ary recursion*.

It would be unreasonable to expect that the advantages listed above should appear manifest in simple examples, since that is where recursion is at its weakest. Consequently we will concentrate in this chapter on explaining recursion and how it works and illustrating some of its characteristics.

1.1 Some simple examples

The simplest example is the factorial function, which is defined by:

$$p! = 1, \qquad\qquad p = 0,$$
$$= 1 \times 2 \times 3 \times \ldots p, \quad p > 0$$

From this definition the function of Fig. 1.1 follows immediately.

Fig. 1.1. A non-recursive function *Fact*.

```
function Fact(p:natural):natural;
  var i,f:natural;
  begin
  f := 1;
  for i := 1 to p do
    f := f*i;
  Fact := f
  end { of function "Fact" };
```

where *natural* is defined as:

> type *natural* = 0 .. *maxint*

In a study of the factorial function one of the first theorems proved is:

$$p! = 1, \qquad\qquad p = 0,$$
$$= p \times (p - 1)!, \quad p > 0$$

from which the function of Fig. 1.2 immediately follows.

Fig. 1.2. A recursive function *Fact*.

```
function Fact(p:natural):natural;
  begin
  if p = 0 then Fact := 1
  else Fact := p*Fact(p-1)
  end { of function "Fact" };
```

Indeed, for many people, the theorem just mentioned *is* the definition. In either case, it must be said that it is hard to argue that either function is more natural than the other.

As a second example, we consider the highest common factor (*HCF*) of two positive integers p and q. A description of Euclid's algorithm for finding the HCF usually goes something like this: 'Divide p by q to give a remainder r. If $r = 0$ then the HCF is q. Otherwise repeat with q and r taking the place of p and q'. From this description the non-recursive version of Fig. 1.3 is usually derived.†

Fig. 1.3. A non-recursive version of *Hcf*.

```
function Hcf(p,q:natural):natural;
  var r:natural;
  begin
  r := p mod q;
  while r <> 0 do
    begin
    p := q;
    q := r;
    r := p mod q
    end;
  Hcf := q
  end { of function "Hcf" };
```

From the same description, the recursive version of Fig. 1.4 follows.

Fig. 1.4. A recursive version of *Hcf*.

```
function Hcf(p,q:natural):natural;
  var r:natural;
  begin
  r := p mod q;
  if r = 0 then Hcf := q
  else Hcf := Hcf(q,r)
  end { of function "Hcf" };
```

This is more natural in the sense that p **mod** q is evaluated in only one place, as in the description, whereas in Fig. 1.3 it is evaluated twice.

† As q must not be 0 we should introduce a type *positive* $= 1 \mathbin{..} maxint$ for it. Since we will give a version later in which q may be 0, we do not do so.

Mathematically we can formulate this as:

$$hcf(p, q) = p, \qquad\qquad p \bmod q = 0,$$
$$= hcf(q, p \bmod q), \quad p \bmod q \neq 0$$

These two examples are fairly well known. As a third example Fig. 1.5 gives a procedure, rather than a function, which prints out an unsigned integer left-justified, that is, with no spaces preceding the most significant digit.

Fig. 1.5. A procedure for writing an unsigned integer left-justified.

```
procedure WriteNatural(i:natural);
  begin
  if i < 10 then
    write(chr(i + ord('0')))
  else
    begin
    WriteNatural(i div 10);
    write(chr(i mod 10 + ord('0')))
    end
  end { of procedure "WriteNatural" };
```

Its action is fairly clear. If i is less than 10, it has only one digit which is printed. If it is greater than 10 (say 375), the procedure is called recursively to print i **div** 10 (here 37) after which the final digit (5) is printed.

1.2 How does recursion work?

The standard run-time storage organisation used in Pascal to ensure the optimal use of store is the *stack*; and this organisation automatically encompasses recursion. We will illustrate this with respect to a program, *Test*, which simply reads x and calls *WriteNatural* to print it. We assume that the *activation record* for a procedure contains, as well as the parameters and local variables, two links. The first, the *return address link (ral)*, holds the address to which control is to be returned on exit from the procedure. The second is called the *stack link (sl)*, because it is used to ensure that the stack returns to the same configuration on exit from a procedure as it had on entry. We assume that the stack is accessed by a set of registers, called the *display*, one register being associated with each textual level. In what follows we call them $D1, D2, \ldots$. On entry to a procedure one of the display registers has to be altered to refer to the variables of this procedure. If the procedure is at level n, then Dn is changed. It is the original value of this register that is the stack link.

5

A procedure call then must:

   (i) stack the return address link,
  (ii) stack the stack link,
 (iii) adjust the display,
 (iv) allocate space for the local variables,
  (v) branch to the code of the called procedure.

The corresponding procedure exit then:

   (i) recovers the space of the local variables,
  (ii) adjusts the display using the stack link,
 (iii) returns to the statement after the call using the return address link.

We illustrate this with respect to the *Test* program mentioned earlier which we give as Fig. 1.6. Note that two points are marked α and β by means of comments.

Fig. 1.6. A program to test *WriteNatural*.

```
program Test(input,output);
type natural = 0..maxint;
var x:natural;

procedure WriteNatural(i:natural);
  begin
  if i < 10 then
    write(chr(i + ord('0')))
  else
    begin
    WriteNatural(i div 10);
    { point β }
    write(chr(i mod 10 + ord('0')))
    end
  end { of procedure "WriteNatural" };

begin
read(x);
write(' The value of ',x:1,' is ');
WriteNatural(x)
{ point α }
end.
```

Suppose we run this program with 375 as data. Within the main program there is only one activation record addressed via $D1$. It contains only the variable x since the concept of links is irrelevant for the main program. After *read(x)* we have:

On entry to *WriteNatural* after the call *WriteNatural*(*x*), an activation record is created for *WriteNatural* containing the links (*ral* and *sl*) and the parameter *i*. It is addressed via *D2*.

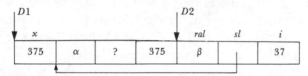

Note that the stack link is irrelevant, since within the main program *D2* is unused.

On the second entry to *WriteNatural*, as a result of the recursive call *WriteNatural*(*i* **div** 10), a further activation record is created for *WriteNatural*. It is accessed via *D2*, while the previous activation record becomes temporarily inaccessible.

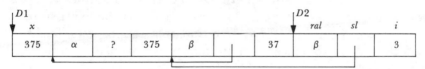

On the third entry to *WriteNatural* we have:

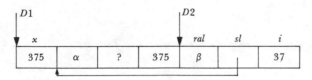

and $chr(i + ord('0'))$, that is the character 3, is then printed.

On exit from this activation of *WriteNatural*, the stack is returned to its previous state so that the second activation record becomes accessible again, and control returns to point *β*.

Then $chr(i \bmod 10 + ord('0'))$, that is, the character 7, is printed.

On exit from this activation we have:

and, as control returns again to point *β*, 5 is printed.

On the exit from the first activation to *WriteNatural* the stack returns to:

and control returns to α, at which point the program stops.

1.3   The storage cost of recursion

From the description of the implementation, the cost in terms of storage associated with recursive procedures is clear. If n is the maximum recursive depth, then the store required is $n \times (p + l + 2)$ where p represents the space required by the parameters and l that required by the local variables. Where the alternative non-recursive solution requires only a small number of local variables for its operation, this cost might be significant. (In the two relevant examples given so far, *Fact* and *Hcf*, n is likely to be small but in Chapter 2 we consider situations where n may be large.)

There are, however, some situations where the non-recursive procedure requires an amount of store which is proportional to n, in which case the comparison between recursive and non-recursive versions may be less clear-cut. In these situations the extra store is used as a stack† and we will assume that some appropriate facilities have been added to Pascal. This is simply a matter of abstraction: the implementation of the facilities in pure Pascal is trivial.

We assume a new structured mode, **stack of**, so that, for example, the declaration:

> **var** s :**stack of** *natural*

declares s to be a stack of natural numbers. This stack is initialised, to an empty stack by:

> **clear** s

Only two accessing statements are available. The first:

> **push** i **onto** s

pushes the value of the expression i onto the top of s, while:

> **pop** i **from** s

pops the top value from s and assigns it to i. Finally:

> s **empty**
> s **not empty**

are predicates which test the state of the stack.

† The term *stack* thus refers to two concepts which are alike in their *first-in*, *last-out* characteristics but have different rules of access.

Fig. 1.7 gives a non-recursive version of *WriteNatural* using these facilities.

Fig. 1.7. A non-recursive version of *WriteNatural*.

```
procedure WriteNatural(i:natural);
  var s:stack of natural;
  begin
  clear s;
  while i >= 10 do
    begin
    push i onto s;
    i := i div 10
    end;
  write(chr(i + ord('0')));
  while s not empty do
    begin
    pop i from s;
    write(chr(i mod 10 + ord('0')))
    end
  end { procedure "WriteNatural" };
```

Clearly in *WriteNatural* the size of the stack will be small†, perhaps 5 or 6, but the general principle is clear: the amount of store required is proportional to the recursive depth, though as there will be fewer links required (here there are none) the constant of proportionality will be smaller than that for the recursive version.

Fig. 1.7 illustrates another point: that the procedures themselves occupy space and the differences in procedure size must be considered. These are generally of a lower order, since there is only one copy of a procedure code, whereas there may be many activation records.

1.4   The time cost of recursion

We indicated in the opening paragraphs of this chapter that even where they have been well written, recursive procedures may run more slowly than their non-recursive counterparts. We illustrate this here by using what is perhaps the most extreme example, the factorial functions given earlier. In Fig. 1.8 we give counts of those of the so-called *structured operations* that are involved: arithmetic, assignment, loop traverse, procedure call and so on.

We also count the number of *elementary operations* by assigning appropriate weights to the structured operations: arithmetic, simple tests and assignments at 1, for-loop entry at 2 (for the assignment

---

† Indeed for this particular example we could avoid the use of a stack by trading space for time, and using quite a different technique.

9

Fig. 1.8. Analysis of the *Fact* functions.

Number of operations of the type	Non-recursive (Fig. 1.1)	Recursive (Fig. 1.2)
Arithmetic	p	$2p$
Assignment	$p+2$	$p+1$
Test		$p+1$
Parameter evaluation	1	$p+1$
Procedure call and exit	1	$p+1$
For-loop entry	1	
For-loop traverse	p	
Elementary operations	$5p+10$	$10p+8$
Elementary operations ($p=10$)	60	108
Time on Cyber 73 ($p=10$)	210 μs	380 μs

and test involved), for-loop traverse at 3 (for the test, increment and assignment involved), parameter evaluation at 1 (for the implied assignment) and procedure call and exit at 5 (for assigning two links and setting the display register on entry, resetting two links on exit). From Fig. 1.8 we see that the recursive procedure is perhaps twice as slow.† This is probably an upper limit on the differences between a linear recursive procedure and the equivalent non-recursive version because the body of *Fact* is quite trivial.

Fig. 1.8 gives as well some timings for the procedures run on a Cyber 73, as do subsequent tables. The figures indicate that the model is a fair approximation to the Cyber Pascal system. The discrepancies arise from the simplicity of the model and from the relative inaccuracy of the timer used.

1.5   Recurrence relations

The analysis of most of the procedures considered in this chapter and the next (those exhibiting linear recursion) is very simple and really needs no formalism. However this is not so with binary and n-ary recursion, and so we will consider an analysis based on the use of a *recurrence relation*. It is convenient to have the notion of the *size* of a problem, so that if T_k represents the cost, however defined, of evaluating a procedure of size k then the recurrence relation defines T_k in terms of the cost of evaluating the smaller problem(s) into which it is broken down. For linear recursion the size is closely related to the recursive depth and T_k is defined in

† This set of weights is very arbitrary and may not be appropriate to some machines and some compilers, particularly where procedures are handled by a subroutine call.

terms of T_{k-1}. A typical recurrence relation, which applies to *Fact*, is:

$$T_k = b + T_{k-1}, \quad k > 0$$
$$ = a, \quad\quad\quad k = 0$$

where a and b are appropriate constants. T_n can be determined quite simply by a process of substitution.

$$T_n = b + T_{n-1}$$
$$ = b + b + T_{n-2}$$
$$ = b \times 2 + T_{n-2}$$
$$\vdots$$
$$ = b \times n + T_0$$
$$ = bn + a$$

This is linear in n which coincides nicely with our use of the phrase linear recursion. It is not the only form of recurrence relation that arises in linear recursion as we shall see. However, in all recurrence relations that do arise, the coefficient of T on the right-hand side is always 1.

1.6 The choice of the explicitly defined case

We want now to consider in the next two sections two aspects which are important in the design of recursive procedures. Firstly the choice of the explicitly defined case. There is often some flexibility in this choice. For example, we have chosen $0! = 1$ as the explicitly defined case in the factorial function. We might have chosen $1! = 1$ as in Fig. 1.9; and provided we always called *Fact* with a parameter >0 it would have operated successfully.

Fig. 1.9. The function *Fact* modified to use $1! = 1$.

```
function Fact(p:natural):natural;
  begin
  if p = 1 then Fact := 1
  else Fact := p*Fact(p-1)
  end { of function "Fact" };
```

But note the implication that two functions for the same problem with different explicitly defined cases are different in that one function might fail in cases where the other does not. For example the evaluation of $Fact(0)$ using Fig. 1.9 would fail as p went out of range!†

---

† As we noted in §1.1 with respect to the parameter q of *Hcf*, it would be better to define p to be of the type *positive*.

Considering the example *Hcf*, if we stop the recursion one step later, that is when $q = 0$ rather than when $p \bmod q = 0$, we produce the elegant function of Fig. 1.10.

Fig. 1.10. A function *Hcf* stopping one step later.

```
function Hcf(p,q:natural):natural;
  begin
  if q = 0 then Hcf := p
  else Hcf := Hcf(q,p mod q)
  end { of function "Hcf" };
```

Note that the local variable r has disappeared. Note, too, that this function gives an interpretation to $Hcf(7, 0)$ where the previous one did not.

The recurrence relation enables us to determine the effect of the change. For the new version of *Fact* we have:

$$T_k = b' + T_{k-1}, \quad k > 1$$
$$= a', \quad\quad\quad k = 1$$

Note we have used constants a' and b' since they will in general be different from a and b, even though this is not true for the factorial functions. The solution is simply:

$$T_n = b'n + (a' - b')$$

Which is the faster depends on the values of a, b, a' and b'. In any event the different will be small. Thus the choice of explicit case is usually made on the grounds of elegance or simplicity or generality. When we consider binary recursion, the difference, however, may turn out to be significant.

1.7 Two-level procedures

The second aspect is the use of *two-level procedures*, in which the main procedure contains within itself a procedure which is recursive and which it calls initially. This technique has a number of advantages which we now consider.

It is clear from the discussion of costs that the number of parameters is significant in that it affects both space and time requirements. Consider a function for evaluating the polynomial:

$$a_0 x^n + a_1 x^{n-1} + \ldots + a_{n-1}x + a_n$$

This is usually evaluated by Horner's method of nested multiplication:

$$(\ldots (((a_0)x + a_1)x + a_2) \ldots + a_{n-1})x + a_n$$

Fig. 1.11 gives a function in which the coefficients are assumed to be in an array a.†

---

† Very often, as here, we will leave some types unspecified, where it is clear what an appropriate definition might be.

Fig. 1.11. A non-recursive version of *Poly*.

```
function Poly(var a:coeff; x:real; n:natural):real;
  var y:real;
      i:natural;
  begin
  y := 0;
  for i := 0 to n do
    y := y*x + a[i];
  Poly := y
  end { of function "Poly" };
```

Note that we have called *a* as a variable even though it serves only to transmit a value to *Poly*. The reason is simply one of efficiency. Since each element of *a* is accessed only once, the cost of copying the whole array (which calling it by value would involve) is more than the cost of the indirect access (which calling as a variable implies). Further we require less space, since here it requires a single location (for the indirect address) whereas it would require space for a copy if it were called by value. We will use this criterion for the choice between call-by-value and call-as-a-variable extensively in this book.

The standard recursive version also follows directly from Horner's re-arrangement as Fig. 1.12 shows.

Fig. 1.12. A recursive version of *Poly*.

```
function Poly(var a:coeff; x:real; n:natural):real;
  begin
  if n = 0 then Poly := a[0]
  else Poly := Poly(a,x,n-1)*x + a[n]
  end { of function "Poly" };
```

Here *a* and *x* are unaltered between calls, and we consume both time and space for them on each recursive call.

To avoid repeatedly assigning these redundant parameters we can use a two-level approach as shown in Fig. 1.13.

Fig. 1.13. The two-level function *Poly*.

```
function Poly(var a:coeff; x:real; n:natural):real;

  function P(k:natural):real;
    begin
    if k = 0 then P := a[0]
    else P := P(k-1)*x + a[k]
    end { of function "P" };

  begin
  Poly := P(n)
  end { of function "Poly" };
```

Here the body of the outer procedure *Poly* contains simply a call to the inner procedure *P* with just the one parameter k which is initialised to n. Within *P* the values of a and x are accessed non-locally. We will use these two-level functions (and procedures) quite extensively in this book and, by convention, we will generally give the inner function (or procedure) a name which is the first letter of the name of the outer one, unless that happens to have a name which starts with a prefix which is common to a group of procedures.

This function certainly uses less space since the inner recursive function has only one parameter. The stack space we require is 5 locations for the outer function plus $3(n + 1)$ for *P*, as against $5(n + 1)$ for the single-level recursive function. (Of course, the non-recursive function requires only 7 locations for the parameters and the local variables.)

An analysis of all three functions is given in Fig. 1.14. It shows that the two-level recursion requires fewer operations than the one-level recursive function, but more than the non-recursive one. However some of the operations involve non-local accesses which the model assumes to be no more costly than local ones. This is a fairly simplistic assumption, and Fig. 1.14 shows that it is not appropriate for the Cyber.

Fig. 1.14. An analysis of the *Poly* functions.

	Wt	Non-recursive (Fig. 1.11)	Recursive (Fig. 1.12)	Two-level (Fig. 1.13)
Arithmetic	1	$2n+2$	$3n$	$3n$
Assignment	1	$n+3$	$n+1$	$n+2$
Subscripting	1	$n+1$	$n+1$	$n+1$
Test	1		$n+1$	$n+1$
Parameter evaluation	1	3	$3n+3$	$n+4$
Procedure call and exit	5	1	$n+1$	$n+2$
For-loop entry	2	1		
For-loop traverse	3	$n+1$		
Elementary operations		$7n+19$	$14n+11$	$12n+18$
Elementary operations ($n=10$)		89	151	138
Time on Cyber 73 ($n=10$)		350 μs	540 μs	540 μs

However the two-level solution has other advantages which are indisputable. Firstly, it enables us to maintain an acceptable interface to the user. For example suppose we wished to write a procedure to evaluate the polynomial:

$$a_0 + a_1 x + a_2 x^2 + \ldots + a_n^n$$

(The one used earlier was $a_0 x^n + a_1 x^{n-1} + \ldots a_n$, so we will call this

PolyUp, reflecting that the coefficients are increasing along the polynomial.) Using Horner's method we evaluate:

$$(\ldots (((a_n)x + a_{n-1})x + a_{n-2}) \ldots + a_1)x + a_0$$

A one-level procedure requires an extra parameter as Fig. 1.15 shows.

Fig. 1.15. A one-level function *PolyUp*.

```
function PolyUp(var a:coeff; x:real; i,n:natural):real;
    begin
    if i = n then PolyUp := a[n]
    else PolyUp := PolyUp(a,x,i+1,n)*x + a[i]
    end { of function "PolyUp" };
```

This means that the user requires an extra (to him, useless) parameter in each call such as *PolyUp* $(a, x, 0, n)$.

The two-level function enables us to retain the usual function heading as shown in Fig. 1.16.

Fig. 1.16. A two-level function *PolyUp*.

```
function PolyUp(var a:coeff; x:real; n:natural):real;

    function P(i:natural):real;
        begin
        if i = n then P := a[n]
        else P := P(i+1)*x + a[i]
        end { of function "P" };

    begin
    PolyUp := P(0)
    end { of function "PolyUp" };
```

Secondly, the use of a two-level solution enables us to accommodate special cases quite simply. Consider a function *Power* whose value is the nth power of x with the added constraint that 0^n is 0. Fig. 1.17 gives a single-level function.

Fig. 1.17. A poor function for *Power*.

```
function Power(x:real; n:integer):real;
    begin
    if x = 0 then Power := 0
    else if n < 0 then Power := 1/Power(x,-n)
    else if n = 0 then Power := 1
    else Power := x*Power(x,n-1)
    end { of function "Power" };
```

Note that on each call x is compared with 0, even though, if it is different from 0 on the first call, it will remain different from 0 for all calls. Similarly n is tested to ensure it is not less than 0 at each

15

call, when, if it were negative initially, its value would have been immediately negated. The two-level solution of Fig. 1.18 avoids this by dealing with these cases in the outer procedure.

Fig. 1.18. A two-level function for *Power*.

```
function Power(x:real; n:integer):real;

    function P(k:natural):real;
      begin
      if k = 0 then P := 1
      else P := x*P(k-1)
      end { of function "P" };

    begin
    if x = 0 then Power := 0
    else if n < 0 then Power := 1/P(-n)
    else Power := P(n)
    end { of function "Power" };
```

Note that this is the recursive equivalent of moving constants outside loops.

1.8   Developing the power example: a cautionary tale

The powering procedures implemented the definition:

$$
\begin{aligned}
x^n &= 0, & x &= 0 \\
&= 1/x^{-n} & x &\neq 0, n < 0 \\
&= 1, & x &\neq 0, n = 0 \\
&= x \times x^{n-1}, & x &\neq 0, n > 0
\end{aligned}
$$

As many readers will have noticed, this procedure is not very efficient for large n. It is $O(n)$ whereas the method often called 'halving and squaring' is $O(\log n)$. This technique calculates x^{14}, for example, by squaring x^7 whereas the original multiplies x by itself 13 times.

Formally we can specify the function:

$$
\begin{aligned}
x^n &= 0, & x &= 0 \\
&= 1/x^{-n}, & x &\neq 0, n < 0 \\
&= 1, & x &\neq 0, n = 0 \\
&= x^{n/2} \times x^{n/2} \times x, & x &\neq 0, n \text{ odd} \\
&= x^{n/2} \times x^{n/2}, & x &\neq 0, n \text{ even and} > 0
\end{aligned}
$$

From this the function of Fig. 1.19 is easily produced.

Fig. 1.19. A faster version of *Power*.

```
function Power(x:real; n:integer):real;

    function P(k:natural):real;
```

```
begin
if k = 0 then P := 1
else if odd(k) then P := sqr(P(k div 2))*x
else P := sqr(P(k div 2))
end { of function "P" };

begin
if x = 0 then Power := 0
else if n < 0 then Power := 1/P(-n)
else Power := P(n)
end { of function "Power" };
```

The analysis of Fig. 1.19 is a little more difficult than those considered previously because of the different actions taken depending on whether k is even or odd. However, the difference is small and we can, as an approximation, assume that k is equally likely to be even or odd. The recurrence relation is:

$$T_k = b + T_{\lfloor k/2 \rfloor}, \quad k > 0$$
$$= a, \qquad\qquad k = 0$$

where $\lfloor k/2 \rfloor$, the *floor* of $k/2$, is the largest integer less than $k/2$. We can solve this for T_n again by simple substitution:

$$T_n = b + T_{\lfloor n/2 \rfloor}$$
$$= b + (b + T_{\lfloor n/4 \rfloor})$$
$$= 2b + T_{\lfloor n/4 \rfloor}$$
$$= 2b + (b + T_{\lfloor n/8 \rfloor})$$
$$= 3b + T_{\lfloor n/8 \rfloor}$$

We can see that, as n is progressively halved, the coefficient of b is increased by 1. Thus we ultimately arrive at:

$$T_n = b\lfloor \log n \rfloor + T_1$$
$$= b\lfloor \log n \rfloor + b + T_0$$
$$= b\lfloor \log n \rfloor + (b + a)$$

This is only the cost of the call of P, of course. We must also add the small cost of the body of *Power*.

This derivation suggests other alternatives, such as stopping the recursion one step earlier (where $k = 1$) and modifying the body of *Power* appropriately. Note that this illustrates another advantage of a two-level procedure: we can stop the recursion earlier without needing to alter the specification. We leave it to the reader to pursue this solution.

We indicated earlier that it is trivially easy to write inefficient recursive procedures. Here is a case in point. Suppose we unthinkingly used explicit multiplication instead of squaring as shown in Fig. 1.20.

Fig. 1.20. A bad version of *Power*.

```
function Power(x:real; n:integer):real;
   function P(k:natural):real;
     begin
     if k = 0 then P := 1
     else if odd(k) then P := P(k div 2)*P(k div 2)*x
     else P := P(k div 2)*P(k div 2)
     end { of function "P" };

   begin
   if x = 0 then Power := 0
   else if n < 0 then Power := 1/P(-n)
   else Power := P(n)
   end { of function "Power" };
```

Unless we have a compiler which can recognise that the multiplications can be replaced by squarings, we find that the procedure is actually worse than the original two-level solution of Fig. 1.18. This is because, at each level, P is called twice. The recurrence relation is:

$$T_k = b + 2T_{\lfloor k/2 \rfloor}, \quad k \neq 0$$
$$= a, \qquad\qquad k = 0$$

whose solution is $(a + b)\bar{n} - a$, where $\bar{n}$ is $2^{\lfloor \log n \rfloor + 1}$, that is the smallest power of 2 which is greater than n.

Fig. 1.21 gives a detailed analysis of these procedures, including the body of *Power*, in which n is the absolute value of the parameter, which is assumed as likely negative as positive.

Fig. 1.21. Analysis of the *Power* functions.

	Wt	One-level (Fig. 1.17)	(Fig. 1.18)	Two-level (Fig. 1.19)	(Fig. 1.20)
Arithmetic	1	$2n+1$	$2n+1$	$2\frac{1}{2}\lfloor \log n \rfloor +3\frac{1}{2}$	$3\bar{n}+n-2$
Assignment	1	$n+1\frac{1}{2}$	$n+2$	$\lfloor \log n \rfloor +3$	$2\bar{n}$
Test	1	$3n+4$	$n+3$	$2 \ \lfloor \log n \rfloor +5$	$3\bar{n}$
Parameter evaluation	1	$2n+3$	$n+3$	$\lfloor \log n \rfloor +4$	$2\bar{n}+1$
Procedure call and exit	5	$n+1\frac{1}{2}$	$n+2$	$\lfloor \log n \rfloor +3$	$2\bar{n}$
Elementary operations		$13n+17$	$10n+19$	$11\frac{1}{2}\lfloor \log n \rfloor +30\frac{1}{2}$	$20\bar{n}+n-1$
Elementary operations $(n=240)$		3137	2419	111	5359
Time on Cyber 73 $(n=240)$		10200 μs	8700 μs	400 μs	20900 μs

18

Note that this small error has changed the order of complexity of the procedure from $O(\log n)$ to $O(n)$. Note, too, that the possibility of such a drastic effect for such a trivial change does not usually occur with iterative procedures.

1.9 Searching

One of the fundamental operations of computer science is searching for an item of a given key in a collection of such items. We assume that the items are of a type *itemtype* defined:

> type *itemtype* = **record**
> > *key* : *keytype*;
> > *info* : *infotype*
> **end**

where both *keytype* and *infotype* are left unspecified.

Let us assume that the items are held in an array whose type is defined by:

> type *sizetype* = 1 .. *max*;
> > *arraytype* = **array** [*sizetype*] **of** *itemtype*

where *max* is an appropriate constant.

Let us assume that the items are not ordered on their keys. In Fig. 1.22 we give an obvious function which proceeds through the array until either the key is found, or all items have been compared.

Fig. 1.22. Searching an array.

```
function InArray(var a:arraytype; n:sizetype; k:keytype):Boolean;

  function I(j:sizetype):Boolean;
    begin
    if k = a[j].key then I := true
    else if j = n then I := false
    else I := I(j+1)
    end { of function "I" };

  begin
  InArray := I(1)
  end { of function "InArray" };
```

On average half the elements will be compared so that the function is $O(n)$.

If the items are held in ascending order of their keys we can do much better by using the method known as *binary-chopping*, which operates as follows. We compare the key of the item being sought with the key of the item in the middle of the array. If it is the smaller, then the item, if it is present, must be in the lower half of the array; otherwise it must be in the upper half. Fig. 1.23 gives an appropriate function.

Fig. 1.23. Binary-chopping.

```
function InArray(var a:arraytype; n:sizetype; k:keytype):Boolean;
  function I(l,u:sizetype):Boolean;
    var mid:sizetype;
    begin
    if l = u then I := k = a[l].key
    else
      begin
      mid := (l+u) div 2;
      if k <= a[mid].key then I := I(l,mid)
      else I := I(mid+1,u)
      end
    end { of function "I" };
  begin
  InArray := I(l,n)
  end { of function "InArray" };
```

Clearly this procedure is $O(\log n)$ since at each stage the size of the array is halved.

1.10 Recursion and reversal

The procedure *WriteNatural* prints out the natural number which is its parameter in the usual way: the procedure *WriteReversedNatural* of Fig. 1.24 prints it out in reverse. That is, if $i = 375$, it prints 573.

Fig. 1.24. A procedure for writing natural numbers reversed.

```
procedure WriteReversedNatural(i:natural);
  begin
  if i < 10 then
    write(chr(i + ord('0')))
  else
    begin
    write(chr(i mod 10 + ord('0')));
    WriteReversedNatural(i div 10)
    end
  end { of procedure "WriteReversedNatural" };
```

The only difference between the procedures is the position of the recursive call: in *WriteNatural* it occurs before the writing of a character, in *WriteReversedNatural* it occurs after. Thus it is often trivial to modify a recursive procedure to produce a reversed form of output – and to accept a reversed form of input. We shall see a useful example in Chapter 2.

With non-recursive procedures the changes are less trivial. In Fig. 1.25 we give an iterative procedure for *WriteReversedNatural*.

Fig. 1.25. A non-recursive version of *WriteReversedNatural*.

```
procedure WriteReversedNatural(i:natural);
  begin
  while i >= 10 do
    begin
    write(chr(i mod 10 + ord('0')));
    i := i div 10
    end;
  write(chr(i + ord('0')))
  end { of procedure "WriteReversedNatural" };
```

The differences between this procedure and the non-recursive version of *WriteNatural*, Fig. 1.7, are manifest. They have quite different structures: *WriteNatural* has two loops while *WriteReversedNatural* has one; and *WriteNatural* requires a stack.

It is an advantage of recursion that a simple change of requirements often involves only a simple change in the procedure.

1.11 Using recursion indirectly

When writing iterative programs, we are accustomed to using concepts which are related to that of the problem and which are useful in its solution. For example, if we are asked to write a procedure for determining whether or not an integer, *n*, is prime, we immediately think of searching (in an organised way) for factors of *n*. If one is found, then *n* is not prime.

A similar strategy is also required with recursive procedures. We cannot write a directly recursive procedure for testing primality, since the primality of *n* cannot be expressed in terms of the primality of $n-1$ (or any other function of *n*). However, we can express the condition *n is prime* as the condition *n has no factors between* 2 *and* $n^{1/2}$. Then we can write this alternative in a way that is directly recursive. Fig. 1.26 gives the resulting two-level function.

Fig. 1.26. A function for determining primality.

```
function Prime(n:natural):Boolean;

  function HasFactors(i:natural):Boolean;
    begin
    if sqr(i) > n then HasFactors := false
    else if n mod i = 0 then HasFactors := true
    else HasFactors := HasFactors(i+1)
    end { of function "HasFactors" };

  begin
  Prime := not HasFactors(2)
  end { of function "Prime" };
```

EXERCISES

1.1 Write a function with the heading:

function *SumCubes* (n : *natural*)

whose value is the sum of the cubes of the integers 1 to n. That is:

$$1^3 + 2^3 + \ldots + n^3$$

1.2 Write a function with the heading:

function *Max* (**var** a : *intarray* ; n : *natural*) : *integer*

whose value is that of the maximum element of the integer array $a[0 \ldots n]$.

1.3 Write a function with the heading:

function *Range* (**var** a : *intarray* ; n : *natural*) : *natural*

whose value is that of the range of the elements of the array a, that is, the difference between the maximum and minimum elements.

1.4 What does the function of Fig. 1.27 do?

Fig. 1.27. A mystery function *X*.

```
function X(var a,b:realarray; n:natural):real;
    begin
    if n = 0 then X := a[0]*b[0]
    else X := X(a,b,n-1) + a[n]*b[n]
    end { of function "X" };
```

1.5 Analyse the function given in Ex. 1.2. Rewrite it non-recursively, analyse the new version and compare it with the original.

1.6 Write a non-recursive procedure *Power* based upon the second definition given in §1.8; analyse it and compare it with the recursive version.

1.7 Fig. 1.28 is a (poorly written) function whose value is that of the maximum element of an integer array.

Fig. 1.28. A poorly written function *Max*.

```
function Max(var a:intarray; n:natural):integer;
    begin
    if n = 0 then Max := a[0]
    else if Max(a,n-1) > a[n] then Max := Max(a,n-1)
    else Max := a[n]
    end { of function "Max" };
```

Analyse the procedure, and compare it with your solution to Ex. 1.2.

1.8 Write a function whose value is that of the continued fraction:

$$a_0 + \cfrac{1}{a_1 + \cfrac{1}{a_2 + \cfrac{{}}{\ddots \cfrac{{}}{a_n}}}}$$

where the coefficients are assumed to be held in array a.

1.9 Solve the recurrence relation (given in §1.8)

$$T_k = b + 2T_{\lfloor k/2 \rfloor}, \quad k \neq 0$$
$$ = a, \quad\quad\quad\ \ k = 0$$

1.10 Improve the *Prime* function of Fig. 1.26 by excluding even numbers greater than 2 from the potential factors tested.

1.11 Write a recursive function to determine whether an integer n is perfect. (A number is perfect if it is equal to the sum of its factors. Thus 6 is perfect because $6 = 3 + 2 + 1$.)

1.12 Write two procedures, one for inserting an item into a sorted array, and one for deleting an item from it.

2

Recursion with linked-linear lists

Some data structures lend themselves naturally to recursion. The simplest of these is the well-known *linked-linear list*, in which a sequence of *nodes* each contains an *item* and a pointer, *next*, to its successor. We shall refer to such a structure as a *list*, and will use throughout the definition:

> **type** *listptr* = ↑*node*;
> *node* = **record**
> *item* :*itemtype*;
> *next* :*listptr*
> **end**

where *itemtype* is, for the moment, left undefined.† The reason that recursive procedures are so appropriate is that the data structure is itself recursively defined: *node* is defined in terms of *listptr* which is itself a pointer to a *node*.

In Pascal, such structures are held in the *heap*, though ultimately some variable pointing to the structure must exist on the stack. Fig. 2.1 gives a diagrammatical representation of a list containing

Fig. 2.1. A simple linked-list structure.

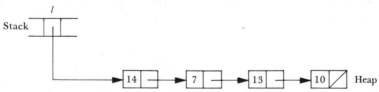

the items 14, 7, 13 and 10 which is pointed to by the variable *l*. Note that within the picture the next field is represented by an

_____
† We will give appropriate definitions from time to time as needed.

arrow pointing to the node, and that a null pointer (found in the last element of the list) is represented by a slash.

2.1 Some simple and general examples

The operations we perform on lists generally depend on the nature of items in the list. There are, though, some operations which are independent of this. Fig. 2.2 gives three: a function *Size* whose value is the number of items in the list, a procedure *WriteList* which writes out the items in the list, using a procedure *WriteItem* to process the individual items, and a procedure *DisposeList* which disposes of the elements of the list.

Figure 2.2. Some simple procedures operating on lists.

```
function Size(l:listptr):natural;
  begin
  if l = nil then Size := 0
  else Size := Size(l↑.next) + 1
  end { of function "Size" };


procedure WriteList(l:listptr);
  begin
  if l <> nil then
    begin
    WriteItem(l↑.item);
    WriteList(l↑.next)
    end
  end { of procedure "WriteList" };


procedure DisposeList(l:listptr);
  begin
  if l <> nil then
    begin
    DisposeList(l↑.next);
    dispose(l)
    end
  end { of procedure "DisposeList" };
```

Clearly the analysis of these procedures follows along the lines of that of Chapter 1, the size of the problem here being the length of the list. We will give no detailed analyses in this chapter, contenting ourselves with *order of magnitude* figures. All the above procedures are $O(|l|)$, where by $|l|$ we mean the size of list l.

The proofs, too, are trivial, using the principle of induction; and so we omit them.

We have expressed the notion of a list in terms of pointers and the heap, because they are the appropriate constructs in Pascal. If a language does not include these notions then they can be simply simulated. We might use two arrays, *item* and *next*, with a given node being held in, say, *item*[*j*], and *next*[*j*]. The array *next* would contain subscripts while *item* would contain the appropriate information. We leave the details of programming the equivalents of, for example, *l*↑.*next* to the reader.

In what follows we return to the original description.

2.2 Copying a list

We give now an example which illustrates the advantage, in terms of simplicity and elegance, of using a recursive procedure to process a recursive data structure. Fig. 2.3 gives a procedure for producing a copy of a list.

Fig. 2.3. A procedure for copying a list.

```
procedure CopyList(var l1:listptr; l2:listptr);
  begin
  if l2 = nil then l1 := nil
  else
    begin
    new(l1);
    l1↑.item := l2↑.item;
    CopyList(l1↑.next,l2↑.next)
    end
  end { of procedure "CopyList" };
```

Its operation is simple: if *l*2 represents an empty list, then the copy must be empty too; otherwise the copy is constructed from a new node containing the first item of *l*2 and a pointer to a copy of the rest of *l*2. This list (*l*2 without its first element) must be copied too, and so we call *CopyList* recursively.

The procedure *CopyList* is a good illustration of the fact that recursive procedures are often easier to write than their non-recursive equivalents. The problem that arises in the non-recursive version of *CopyList* (and indeed in any procedure with a *listptr* parameter called as a variable) is illustrated by Fig. 2.4 which shows the store part-way through creating in *cl* a copy of *l*. Suppose the first two items of the copy had been created as shown. Then in creating the third item, we need a pointer, *p* say, which points to its predecessor (the second node) so that its *next* field can be assigned. The problem arises in creating the first node, since it has no predecessor. Fig. 2.5

Fig. 2.4. Creating a copy of a list.

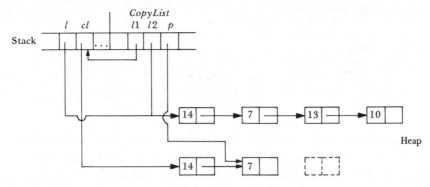

gives one of the standard solutions in which the first node is treated specially.

Fig. 2.5. A non-recursive procedure for copying a list.

```
procedure CopyList(var l1:listptr; l2:listptr);
  var p:listptr;
  begin
  if l2 = nil then l1 := nil
  else
    begin
    new(l1);
    l1↑.item := l2↑.item;
    p := l1; l2 := l2↑.next;
    while l2 <> nil do
      begin
      new(p↑.next);
      p↑.next↑.item := l2↑.item;
      p := p↑.next; l2 := l2↑.next
      end;
    p↑.next := nil
    end
  end { of procedure "CopyList" };
```

In this context we often talk of *p* as being a *trailing pointer* since it always trails one node behind the node being created. Often too, we use two pointers, one pointing to the newly created node, and one trailing behind (like *p* is in the above). A two-pointer version can be found in Alagic and Arbib (1978).

An alternative non-recursive version of *CopyList* is given in Fig. 2.6.

Fig. 2.6. Another non-recursive procedure for copying a list.

```
procedure CopyList(var l1:listptr; l2:listptr);
  var p:listptr;
  begin
  new(l1); p := l1;
  while l2 <> nil do
```

27

```
    begin
    new(p↑.next);
    p↑.next↑.item := 12↑.item;
    p := p↑.next; 12 := 12↑.next
    end;
  p↑.next := nil;
  p := 11; 11 := 11↑.next; dispose(p)
  end { of procedure "CopyList" };
```

The procedure simply creates a dummy as the first node of $l1$; produces the copy such that it is pointed to by $l1\uparrow.next$; and finally beheads $l1$. The two non-recursive procedures are of about the same speed, size and complexity. They are both, however, more opaque than the recursive one. (It is an interesting exercise at this point to close this book and attempt to re-create all three procedures.)

The action of adding an item at the head of a list (including the empty list) occurs so frequently in what follows, that we will use an abbreviation. The statement:

$\qquad NewList(l1,i,l2)$

causes a node with item i to be added at the head of the list $l2$ and calls this extended list $l1$. It is short for:

$\qquad new(temp)$;
$\qquad temp\uparrow.item := i; temp\uparrow.next := l2$;
$\qquad l1 := temp$

Note that the third parameter $l2$ may be the same as the first, $l1$, or be **nil**.

The action of deleting the element at the head of a list, called beheading, occurs frequently, too. We introduce the statement:

$\qquad Behead(l)$

as a shorthand for:

$\qquad temp := l$;
$\qquad l := l\uparrow.next$;
$\qquad dispose(temp)$

Note that l acts as if it were a parameter called as a variable so that, for example, $Behead(l\uparrow.next)$ will delete the second node of l rather than its first. $Behead$, then, is a general sequence for node deletion.

2.3   Lists used to hold sequences

Because of their generality, lists have a wide range of uses. In this section we will consider them as sequences and assume, as in Chapter 1:

```
type itemtype = record
                  key :keytype;
                  info :infotype
                end
```

where both *keytype* and *infotype* are still left unspecified. Further we assume the items are unordered.

The classical operations required on a sequence are to determine whether an item with a given key is in the sequence (and maybe to indicate where it is), to insert an item, and to delete an item with a given key (if it is there).

Fig. 2.7 gives appropriate procedures for searching and deleting which, for efficiency reasons, are written using two levels. Note that in *DeleteFromList* the list *l* is called as a variable. This is because the act of deletion may eliminate the first node of the list and therefore *l* must be altered to point to the new first node. The reader who has little experience with pointer variables and parameters called as variables will do well to study this procedure carefully, simulating it by hand if necessary. Similar procedures occur throughout this chapter.

Fig. 2.7. The basic procedures for (unordered) sequences.

```
function InList(l:listptr; k:keytype):Boolean;

   function I(l:listptr):Boolean;
     begin
     if l = nil then I := false
     else if k = l↑.item.key then I := true
     else I := I(l↑.next)
     end { of function "I" };

   begin
   InList := I(l)
   end { of function "InList" };


procedure DeleteFromList(var l:listptr; k:keytype);

   procedure D(var l:listptr);
     begin
     if l = nil then { item not there }
     else if k = l↑.item.key then Behead(l)
     else D(l↑.next)
     end { of procedure "D" };

   begin
   D(l)
   end { of procedure "DeleteFromList" };
```

The analysis of these procedures must be a statistical one since the time taken depends on the data. On average, one half of the items must be scanned so that the procedures are still $O(n)$.

Since we have assumed that the sequences are not ordered on their keys, the process of insertion is likely to depend on the application. If the items are to be stored in the order in which they are inserted, then *NewList* does all that is required; if a check has to be made that an item has not already been inserted then a procedure along the lines of *InList* is needed.

These procedures also illustrate the strength of recursion. Let us consider *InList*, and in particular the recursive procedure *I* nested within it. This function terminates either when $l = $ nil (in which case the item is not there) or when $k = l\uparrow.item.key$ (in which case it is). A non-recursive version must test this conjunction of conditions in a loop. But $(l = $ nil$)$ or $(k = l\uparrow.item.key)$ is undefined when $l = $ nil and on many systems will cause the program to be terminated. The traditional solution is to introduce a Boolean variable *found* which is used to hold appropriate values of $k = l\uparrow.item.key$, as shown in Fig. 2.8.

Fig. 2.8. The traditional non-recursive version of *InList*.

```
function InList(l:listptr; k:keytype):Boolean;
  var found:Boolean;
  begin
  found := false;
  while (l <> nil) and not found do
    begin
    found := k = l↑.item.key;
    l := l↑.next
    end;
  InList := found
  end { of function "InList" };
```

While many readers will have written just such procedures, not having been introduced to recursion, it is difficult to argue that they are natural. As Fig. 2.8 demonstrates, quite different treatments are accorded to the two terminating conditions. A more elegant solution arises from simulating Zahn's construct (1974) by state variables as advocated by Atkinson (1978). Fig. 2.9 gives *InList* wirtten this way.

Fig. 2.9. The function *InList* with state variables.

```
function InList(l:listptr; k:keytype):Boolean;
  var state:(searching,notthere,found);
  begin
  state := searching;
```

```
repeat
  if l = nil then state := notthere
  else if k = l↑.item.key then state := found
  else l := l↑.next
until state <> searching;
InList := state = found
end { of function "InList" };
```

Note that this function is closely related to the recursive one – indeed it would be hard to separate the two on the score of naturalness. The non-recursive version has a small disadvantage in that it introduces the notion of a state variable whereas the recursive version does not.

2.4   Lists as ordered sequences

We have assumed so far that the items in a list are unordered. There are situations in which it is desirable to maintain the items in ascending sequence, say, of their keys. This means that searching and deletion need not scan the whole list but may stop when an item with a key larger than that of the item being sought is found. There is only one sensible insertion procedure now (to insert in sequence) and an appropriate procedure is included in Fig. 2.10 which gives the three basic procedures for searching, insertion and deletion.

Fig. 2.10. The basic procedures for ordered sequences.

```
function InList(l:listptr; k:keytype):Boolean;

  function I(l:listptr):Boolean;
    begin
    if l = nil then I := false
    else if k = l↑.item.key then I := true
    else if k < l↑.item.key then I := false
    else I := I(l↑.next)
    end { of function "I" };

  begin
  InList := I(l)
  end { of function "InList" };


procedure InsertInList(var l:listptr; it:itemtype);

  procedure I(var l:listptr);
    begin
    if l = nil then NewList(l,it,nil)
    else if it.key = l↑.item.key then { item already there }
    else if it.key < l↑.item.key then NewList(l,it,l)
    else I(l↑.next)
    end { of procedure "I" };
```

```
      begin
      I(1)
      end { of procedure "InsertInList" };


   procedure DeleteFromList(var l:listptr; k:keytype);

      procedure D(var l:listptr);
         begin
         if l = nil then { item not there }
         else if k = l↑.item.key then Behead(l)
         else if k < l↑.item.key then { item not there }
         else D(l↑.next)
         end { of procedure "D" };

      begin
      D(1)
      end { of procedure "DeleteFromList" };
```

2.5   An example: polynomials

In many situations the elements of a list are processed in an organised way so that insertions and deletions take place not at random throughout the list but at a position marked by a pointer into the list. We use an example due to Alagic and Arbib (1978).

Suppose we represent a polynomial in t by a list in which the items consist of the *power* of t for a given term and its *coefficient* assumed to be integer. Thus we have:

> type *itemtype* = record
> > *coeff*:*integer*;
> > *power*:*natural*
> > end

Suppose, too, that the terms are stored with the powers in descending order of magnitude. Thus the polynomial:

$$3x^4 + 5x^3 + 2x - 2$$

is stored as in Fig. 2.11.

Fig. 2.11. The representation of $3x^4 + 5x^3 + 2x - 2$.

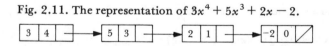

We wish to write procedures to operate on these polynomials; for example, to add two of them. To give further variety to the examples we follow Alagic and Arbib (1978) and give a procedure in Fig. 2.12 which adds one polynomial $l2$ to another $l1$.

32

Fig. 2.12. A procedure for polynomial addition.

```
procedure PolyAdd(var l1:listptr; l2:listptr);
  begin
  if l1 = nil then CopyList(l1,l2)
  else if l2 = nil then { do nothing }
  else if l1↑.item.power > l2↑.item.power then PolyAdd(l1↑.next,l2)
  else if l1↑.item.power = l2↑.item.power then
    begin
    l1↑.item.coeff := l1↑.item.coeff + l2↑.item.coeff;
    PolyAdd(l1↑.next,l2↑.next);
    if l1↑.item.coeff = 0 then Behead(l1)
    end
  else { if l1↑.item.power < l2↑.item.power then }
    begin
    NewList(l1,l2↑.item,l1);
    PolyAdd(l1↑.next,l2↑.next)
    end
  end { of procedure "PolyAdd" };
```

The procedures we have considered up until now have been so straightforward that there seemed no need to give an English description. The *PolyAdd* procedure is a little more complicated as are the ones which follow. We could create a formalism such as that used to describe the power procedures in Chapter 1. Since such a formalism would be closely related to the Pascal procedure, we will not do so. Instead we give a brief description.

The action when one or other of the lists is empty is easily described. If $l1$ refers to an empty list, then a copy of $l2$ must be made and assigned to it. If, on the other hand, $l2$ is empty, then $l1$ already contains the sum and no further action is required.

When neither list is empty then the action required depends on the relative values of the *power* field of the items at the head of the two lists. There are three cases:

(i) The *power* field of $l1$ is larger than that of $l2$. This item of $l1$ forms part of the sum; and we polyadd $l2$ to the rest of $l1$.

(ii) The *power* fields of $l1$ and $l2$ are equal. An item with the same *power* field will be part of the sum, with its *coeff* field the sum of the *coeff* fields of $l1$ and $l2$, except when that sum is 0. We then polyadd the rest of both lists.

(iii) The *power* field of $l1$ is smaller than that of $l2$. An item with the same value as that of $l2$ is added to $l1$, and we polyadd the rest of $l2$ to $l1$.

Clearly the procedure is $O(|l1| + |l2|)$.

This procedure illustrates two small time inefficiencies of recursion not so far met. Firstly, this procedure has two parameters which must, of course, be assigned on each call. However, on many calls only one parameter is changed. We can capitalise on this very easily in a non-recursive procedure, but not in a recursive one. The extension of the two-level technique produces far too involved a procedure. Secondly, the non-recursive version can easily be adapted to cater efficiently for the situation where the sum contains long sequences of terms from $l1$ and $l2$ alternatively. Whether this is significant or not is open to question. The reader who wishes to pursue the matter is referred to Alagic and Arbib (1978) for a closely related non-recursive version.

2.6 Lists as sets

Lists are often used to represent sets. A set can be thought of as a sequence with certain additional properties:

(i) The order of the elements is irrelevant;

(ii) Items have no keys;

(iii) No item appears twice.

Since the order of items is irrelevant we are free to choose an ordering which will make the operations we propose to perform the most efficient. In some situations we may use unordered lists – in others we may choose ordered ones. In either case the fundamental operations of searching, deleting and inserting are applicable; as are the procedures of §2.2 and §2.3. So, too, are the classical set operations of union, intersection and set difference, and the test for a subset. Fig. 2.13 gives a procedure for set union, which assumes that the sets are represented by ordered lists. Note that in contrast to *PolyAdd* this procedure has three parameters, and that the union of $l2$ and $l3$ is assigned to $l1$.

Fig. 2.13. A procedure for set union.

```
procedure Union(var l1:listptr; l2,l3:listptr);
  begin
  if l2 = nil then CopyList(l1,l3)
  else if l3 = nil then CopyList(l1,l2)
  else if l2↑.item < l3↑.item then
    begin
    NewList(l1,l2↑.item,nil);
    Union(l1↑.next,l2↑.next,l3)
    end
  else if l2↑.item = l3↑.item then
    begin
    NewList(l1,l2↑.item,nil);
    Union(l1↑.next,l2↑.next,l3↑.next)
    end
  else { if l2↑.item > l3↑.item then }
```

34

```
      begin
      NewList(l1,l3↑.item,nil);
      Union(l1↑.next,l2,l3↑.next)
      end
   end { of procedure "Union" };
```

Mathematically we define the union of sets $l2$ and $l3$:

$$l2 \cup l3 = \{x \mid x \in l2 \lor x \in l3\}$$

Since the elements held within $l1$ and $l2$ are in ascending order we can rephrase this in terms of the operator $\rightarrow$ meaning *insert as the first element of*, whose first operand is an item and whose second is a set. Using *first*(l) to refer to the item at the head of the list and *rest*(l) as the list l after beheading we have:

$$
\begin{aligned}
l2 \cup l3 &= l3, & l2 &= \{\ \} \\
&= l2, & l3 &= \{\ \} \\
&= first(l2) \rightarrow rest(l2) \cup l3, & first(l2) &< first(l3) \\
&= first(l2) \rightarrow rest(l2) \cup rest(l3), & first(l2) &= first(l3) \\
&= first(l3) \rightarrow l2 \cup rest(l3), & first(l2) &> first(l3)
\end{aligned}
$$

Fig. 2.13 is a direct implementation of this definition.

Each recursive call produces an element of $l1$. (This is true, too, of the calls within *CopyList*.) Thus the procedure is $O(|l1|)$ which, in the worst case is $O(|l2| + |l3|)$.

Fig. 2.14 gives a function *Subset* whose value is true if its first parameter, $l1$, is a subset of its second, $l2$. Its action is obvious.

Fig. 2.14. A function for *Subset*.

```
function Subset(l1,l2:listptr):Boolean;
   begin
   if l1 = nil then Subset := true
   else if l2 = nil then Subset := false
   else if l1↑.item < l2↑.item then
     Subset := false
   else if l1↑.item = l2↑.item then
     Subset := Subset(l1↑.next,l2↑.next)
   else { if l1↑.item > l2↑.item then }
     Subset := Subset(l1,l2↑.next)
   end { of function "Subset" };
```

The procedures for intersection and set difference follow similar lines to that for union.

2.7   A larger example: multi-length arithmetic

The integers of Pascal have a range restricted by the word size of the computer on which the program is being run. Usually this range is perfectly adequate, but there are situations where it is not. For example, if we wish to know 100! or the 500th Fibonacci number or the smallest prime greater than 10^{100}, we need integers of a much larger range. We consider now the creation of a package of procedures for performing arithmetic on integers of arbitrarily large precision.

An obvious method of storing the integers is to use a list with each item storing a part of the number. We could store one decimal digit to a word, but a more efficient solution would be to store as many digits as possible. The number of digits is constrained by the fact that we must perform operations on them using the normal integer arithmetic facilities. Thus, because of multiplication, the size of the items must be less than the square root of the largest Pascal integer available on the machine. For a 16-bit machine this means two digits per word, for example. In the following procedures we use the constant *base* to represent one more than the largest integer in an item. (The choice of the word *base* reflects the fact that with a two-digit item, for instance, we are effectively doing base-100 arithmetic.) We need, as well, to store the sign of a number, and we will also find it convenient to store its size (the number of items it contains). Thus an appropriate definition might be:

> **type** *signtype* = (*plus*,*minus*);
>   *multi* = **record**
>   *sign* : *signtype*;
>   *size* : *natural*;
>   *value* : *listptr*
>   **end**

Fig. 2.15 shows the storage of the variable m which represents -1048576 assuming $base = 100$, where we have made the decision to store the items with the least significant digits at the head of the list. It would have been possible, of course, to store them the other way round.

Fig. 2.15. The multi-length integer -1048576.

The design of a full package is not possible within the space available here (and is left to a project at the end of the chapter).

36

Instead we sketch out a package and give some illustrative examples. As well as the *DisposeList* procedure (Fig. 2.2) we need procedures for input and output, for converting to and from normal integers, for comparison and for the fundamental arithmetic operations.

Let us suppose we have chosen to have a single comparison procedure, which mimics the hardware operation often available on machines, rather than six functions, which correspond to the relational operators of Pascal. That is, we assume the definition:

> type *relation* = (*lt*,*eq*,*gt*)

and a procedure with the heading:

> procedure *MultiCompare*(var *r*:*relation*; *m*1,*m*2:*multi*)

which sets *r* according to whether *m*1 is less than, equal to, or greater than *m*2. We note immediately that only where the two numbers have the same size and sign need we consider their value. Fig. 2.16 gives an appropriate procedure.

Fig. 2.16. A procedure for comparing multi-length integers.

```
procedure MultiCompare(var r:relation; m1,m2:multi);

  procedure C(l1,l2:listptr);
    begin
    if l1 = nil then r := eq
    else
      begin
      C(l1↑.next,l2↑.next);
      if r = eq then
        if l1↑.item < l2↑.item then r := lt
        else if l1↑.item > l2↑.item then r := gt
      end
    end { of procedure "C" };

  begin
  if m1.sign <> m2.sign then
    if m1.sign = plus then r := gt else r := lt
  else if m1.size <> m2.size then
    if (m1.size > m2.size) = (m1.sign=plus) then
        r := gt else r := lt
  else if m1.sign = plus then
    C(m1.value,m2.value)
  else
    C(m2.value,m1.value)
  end { of procedure "MultiCompare" };
```

The internal procedure *C* is an interesting one. Remember that a number is stored with its least significant digits at the head of the list. To effect the comparison we need to access the most significant digits first. Thus the procedure must first get to the end of the lists, deem two null lists to be equal, and, as long as the numbers remain equal, compare pairs of items back towards the head of the list.

As we noted in §1.10, a subsequent decision to reverse the order in which we hold the items means that only a small change to C is required. The new version is given in Fig. 2.17.

Fig. 2.17. A version of C assuming the reverse order of items.

```
procedure C(l1,l2:listptr);
  begin
  if l1 = nil then r := eq
  else if l1↑.item > l2↑.item then r := gt
  else if l1↑.item < l2↑.item then r := lt
  else C(l1↑.next,l2↑.next)
  end { of procedure "C" };
```

This is obviously a neater and faster procedure than the earlier one, and this might incline us to reverse he original decision about the order of storing the digits. However, the effect of such a decision on the procedures for performing the arithmetic must be considered too. We leave this as an exercise at the end of the chapter.

These arithmetic procedures are rather more complicated. We consider here only the procedure of the heading:

procedure $MultiAdd$(var $m1:multi$; $m2,m3:multi$)

which sets $m1$ to the sum of $m2$ and $m3$. As we have chosen a sign-and-modulus representation we have the problem, famil r to us all, of adding numbers of different sign. In normal decim l usage to add -46 to 73, say, or to 27 we have to subtract the moduli (the right way round). Rather than recite the rules, we give the procedure of Fig. 2.18 which is expressed in terms of the procedures $AddMods$, which adds the moduli of two numbers, $SubMods$ which subtracts the moduli and $Zero$ (which creates a zero result).

Note that as $MultiCompare$ compares signed numbers and we want here to compare moduli, we must first make the numbers positive before calling $MultiCompare$. Note, too, that the list originally referred to by $m1$ must be deleted.

Fig. 2.18. A procedure for adding two multi-length numbers.

```
procedure MultiAdd(var m1:multi; m2,m3:multi);
  var s2,s3:signtype;
      r:relation;
      old:listptr;
  begin
  old := m1.value;
  if m2.sign = m3.sign then
```

```
      begin
      ml.sign := m2.sign;
      AddMods(ml,m2,m3)
      end
   else { if m2.sign <> m3.sign then }
      begin
      s2 := m2.sign; s3 := m3.sign;
      m2.sign := plus; m3.sign := plus;
      MultiCompare(r,m2,m3);
      case r of
      lt:begin
         ml.sign := s3;
         SubMods(ml,m3,m2)
         end { of case "lt" };
      eq:Zero(ml);
      gt:begin
         ml.sign := s2;
         SubMods(ml,m2,m3)
         end { of case "gt" }
      end { of cases on "r" }
      end;
   DisposeList(old)
   end { of procedure "MultiAdd" };
```

The procedure *Zero* is trivial: it simply sets the fields of its parameters to *plus*, 0, **nil** respectively. The procedures *AddMods* and
SubMods are more substantial.

It is convenient when adding two numbers of different length, for
the augend to be the larger, and the body of *AddMods* arranges this.
The inner procedure *A* actually performs the addition. The advantage
of storing the numbers with their least significant digits at the head
becomes manifest when we consider addition, because we must
start adding at the least significant end. The procedure *A* does this,
taking care of any carry which may take place. Note that its parameters are quite different from those of *AddMods*, being pointers
to the parts of the numbers not yet added, together with the carry.

Fig. 2.19. A procedure for adding the moduli of two multi-length
integers.

```
procedure AddMods(var ml:multi; m2,m3:multi);
   type carry = 0..1;

   procedure A(var l1:listptr; l2,l3:listptr; c:carry);
      var sum:integer;
         next13:listptr;
      begin
      if l2 = nil { in which case l3 = nil } then
         if c = 1 then
```

39

```
      begin
      NewList(l1,1,nil);
      ml.size := ml.size + 1
      end
    else { do nothing }
  else { if 12 <> nil then }
    begin
    if 13 = nil then
      begin
      sum := 12↑.item + c;
      next13 := nil
      end
    else { if 13 <> nil then }
      begin
      sum := 12↑.item + 13↑.item + c;
      next13 := 13↑.next
      end;
    NewList(l1,sum mod base,nil);
    A(11↑.next,12↑.next,next13,sum div base)
    end
  end { of procedure "A" };

begin
ml.value := nil;
if m2.size > m3.size then
  begin
  ml.size := m2.size;
  A(ml.value,m2.value,m3.value,0)
  end
else
  begin
  ml.size := m3.size;
  A(ml.value,m3.value,m2.value,0)
  end
end { of procedure "AddMods" };
```

The procedure *SubMods* follows similar lines though, by definition, the minuend is never shorter than the subtrahend. We leave completion of the package to the reader.

2.8 Iteration and linear recursion

In these first two chapters we have given a number of non-recursive procedures. The early ones, *Fact* and *Hcf*, were given basically as background. The later ones, such as both versions of *CopyList*, and *InList*, were used to illustrate the 'naturalness' of their recursive equivalents. We now consider the causes of the 'unnaturalness' of the non-recursive versions.

Note that most linear recursive procedures fall into one of two classes according to whether the processing takes place before or after the recursive call. If it comes before, the procedure is said to be a *preorder* one. The phrase *tail recursion* is often applied too as a consequence of the recursive call being the last action of the procedure. If the processing comes after the recursive call we refer to the procedure as a *postorder* one. This classification is clearer if we use formal procedures instead of functions, and in Fig. 2.20 we give schemata relevant to these two classes.

Fig. 2.20. A *'PreOrder'* and a *'PostOrder'* schema.

```
procedure PreOrder(x:xtype);
  begin
  if P(x) then M(x)
  else
    begin
    S1(x);
    PreOrder(F(x))
    end
  end { of procedure "PreOrder" };


procedure PostOrder(x:xtype);
  begin
  if P(x) then M(x)
  else
    begin
    PostOrder(F(x));
    S2(x)
    end
  end { of procedure "PostOrder" };
```

In this figure:

x represents the parameters
$P(x)$ is a Boolean expression in x
$M(x)$ ⎫
$S1(x)$ ⎬ are statements involving x
$S2(x)$ ⎭
$F(x)$ is a function of x

These two schemata do not cover all cases, of course. Some procedures, such as C of Fig. 2.17, have more complex conditions which cannot be expressed in this simple form. Furthermore some procedures process both before and after the recursive call. Nevertheless this classification of preorder and postorder is a useful one.

The 'unnaturalness' of non-recursive procedures arises from three causes:

(i) Postorder procedures generally (but not always) require a stack and this adds a new concept to the problem.

(ii) Procedures which create or alter list structures need a variable parameter – and the simulation of this parameter in a non-recursive procedure adds a further problem.

(iii) Because of the way in which the evaluation of a Boolean expression is defined, we have to be very careful when expressing the loop that is required in a non-recursive version. We have to introduce either a Boolean variable or a state variable to avoid the evaluation of an undefined expression.

These problems are generally enough to convince us of the desirability of a recursive version. However, if we have a preorder procedure which only inspects a list, then causes (i) and (ii) are not relevant. In this situation, a procedure based on iteration is fairly simple to write – and is certainly fairly 'natural'.

Though we prefer to use the recursive version (and will do so throughout this book), there is one situation in which we will resort to an iterative approach. This is when different recursive forms occur in a procedure. If one of these is linear preorder, and has no complications due to variable parameters, the iterative form is used.

2.9 More complex data structures

There is one further advantage of using recursive procedures. When we discussed copying lists in §2.2 we gave two non-recursive versions. One of these involved initially adding a dummy item at the head of the list, and subsequently, after the copying had been done, deleting this dummy item. This continual introduction and elimination of the dummy item is undoubtedly inefficient, and if we were obliged to write a set of iterative procedures to process sequences held in a list, we would most certainly make this dummy a permanent part of each list. We would then call it a *header*. Procedures such as copying, searching, deleting and so on would be those given earlier, with the initial *NewList* and final *Behead* statements eliminated. An empty list would consist simply of a header; so that, for example, testing for an empty list would be more complicated than before.

Fig. 2.21. A circular list with header.

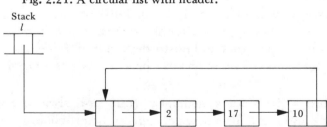

Thus the further advantage of recursion is that we do not need to consider specially modified data structures.

Sentinels are still useful in searching applications and sometimes this leads to a slighly more complex structure. For example, we can introduce a header, and, by making the list circular, use it to hold a sentinel. For example, Fig. 2.21 gives the list $l = (2, 17, 10)$.

A function *InList* for searching the list is given in Fig. 2.22. It should be compared with the function of Fig. 2.7.

Fig. 2.22. Searching a circular list with header.

```
function InList(1:listptr; k:keytype):Boolean;

   function I(11:listptr):Boolean;
     begin
     if k = 11↑.item.key then I := 11 <> 1
     else I := I(11↑.next)
     end { of function "I" };

   begin
   1↑.item.key := k;
   InList := I(1↑.next)
   end { of function "InList" };
```

EXERCISES

2.1 Write a function that counts the number of items of a given key on a list.

2.2 Write a procedure with the heading:
procedure *Reverse* (var $l1: listptr; l2: listptr$)
which sets $l1$ to point to a list whose elements are those of $l2$ but in reverse order.

2.3 Write a modified version of the *PolyAdd* procedure of Fig. 2.12 with the heading:
procedure *PolyAdd*(var $l1: listptr; l2, l3: listptr$);
which sets $l1 = l2 + l3$.

2.4 Rewrite the *PolyAdd* procedure of Ex. 2.3 non-recursively.

2.5 Write a procedure *PolyMult* to multiply two polynomials held as in Fig. 2.11.

2.6 Write a procedure with the heading:
procedure *Intersection* (var $l1: listptr; l2, l3: listptr$)
which sets $l1 = l2 \cap l3$ assuming the sets to be ordered.

2.7 Write an alternative procedure for *Intersection* which assumes the sets are unordered. What is its order of complexity?

2.8 Recast the procedure *Intersection* non-recursively.

2.9 Write a complete package for multi-length arithmetic, and use it to find 100! and the 500th Fibonacci number. (You may, after reading Chapter 4, want to rewrite the Fibonacci part.)

2.10 Investigate the effects on the multi-length arithmetic package of:
  (i) reversing the order in which the digits are stored, and
  (ii) using a complements form of representing negative numbers.

3
Recursion with binary trees

In Chapter 2 we considered linked-linear list structures defined by:

> **type** *listptr* = ↑*node*;
>   *node* = **record**
>   *item* :*itemtype*;
>   *next* : *listptr*
>   **end**

When processing list structures, the elements were accessed in a strictly sequential manner since each item had only one successor, that defined by *next* - except, of course, for the last item which had none.

We are going to consider in this chapter the *binary tree*, a structure which arises when we allow an item to have up to two successors. The definition we shall use is:

> **type** *treeptr* = ↑*node*;
>   *node* = **record**
>   *left* :*treeptr*;
>   *item* :*itemtype*;
>   *right* :*treeptr*
>   **end**

The use of the identifiers *left* and *right* as pointers to the two successors is traditional and reflects the way we generally draw trees.

We will find, when processing such trees, that sometimes linear recursive procedures are adequate, but that on other occasions we require *binary recursion*. That is, an invocation of a recursive procedure will involve two further invocations.

3.1 Binary search trees

One very important application of binary trees is found in searching and sorting problems, in which case the trees are often called *search trees*.

In Fig. 3.1 we give two such trees holding the mnemonic function codes for a hypothetical computer. Note that it is conventional not to draw a box around each node, nor to add an arrow-head on the branches, which always point down, nor to mark **nil** pointers.

Fig. 3.1. Two binary search trees.

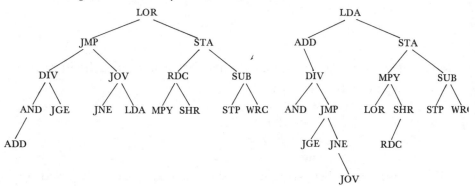

The item will usually contain a *key* together with other *info*rmation so that, as in Chapter 2, we define *itemtype* as:

    type *itemtype* = record
                key : *keytype*;
                info : *infotype*
            end

For the sake of simplicity we omitted the *info* field in Fig. 3.1.

The distinguishing characteristic of the search tree is that, for each node, the keys of all the items on its left branch are less than the key of the item at the node itself, which, in turn, is less than the keys of all the items on the right branch. If we interpret *is less than* as *alphabetically precedes* then the two trees of Fig. 3.1 are obviously search trees.

The significance of search trees lies in the speed with which the operations of searching, inserting and deleting can, in general, be accomplished. This is because, if an item is not at a node, one test determines whether to follow its left or right branch, depending on whether the key of the item is less than or greater than the key of the item at a node. If the two branches are of more or less the same size, then at each stage this test effectively halves the number of nodes to be subsequently considered.

In Fig. 3.2 we give the classical operations which we will consider in turn. Note that we have introduced a statement typified by:

$NewTree(t,l,i,r)$

as a shorthand for a sequence to create a new node of a tree pointed to by t with fields l, i and r respectively. This is clearly analogous to $NewList(l1,i,l2)$ of Chapter 2 and is used in similar situations.

Fig. 3.2. The basic procedures for search trees.

```
function OnTree(t:treeptr; k:keytype):Boolean;

    function O(t:treeptr):Boolean;
      begin
      if t = nil then O := false
      else if k = t↑.item.key then O := true
      else if k < t↑.item.key then O := O(t↑.left)
      else { if k > t↑.item.key then } O := O(t↑.right)
      end { of function "O" };

    begin
    OnTree := O(t)
    end { of function "OnTree" };


procedure InsertOnTree(var t:treeptr; it:itemtype);

    procedure I(var t:treeptr);
      begin
      if t = nil then NewTree(t,nil,it,nil)
      else if it.key = t↑.item.key then { item already there }
      else if it.key < t↑.item.key then I(t↑.left)
      else { if it.key > t↑.item.key then } I(t↑.right)
      end { of procedure "I" };

    begin
    I(t)
    end { of procedure "InsertOnTree" };


procedure DeleteFromTree(var t:treeptr; k:keytype);
    var temp:treeptr;
    begin
    if t = nil then
      { item not there }
    else if k = t↑.item.key then
      begin
      if t↑.left = nil then
        begin { cases (i) and (ii) }
        temp := t; t := t↑.right; dispose(temp)
        end
```

47

```
        else if t↑.right = nil then
      begin { case (iii) }
      temp := t; t:= t↑.left; dispose(temp)
      end
    else { if (t↑.left <> nil) and (t↑.right <> nil) then }
      begin { case (iv) }
      FindPredecessor(temp,t);
      t↑.item := temp↑.item;
      DeleteFromTree(t↑.left,t↑.item.key)
      end
    end { of actual deletion sequence }
  else if k < t↑.item.key then
    DeleteFromTree(t↑.left,k)
  else { if k > t↑.item.key then }
    DeleteFromTree(t↑.right,k)
  end { of procedure "DeleteFromTree" };
```

We noted in Chapter 2 the similarity of the sequences for searching, inserting and deleting in an ordered list. The same is true for the sequences of Fig. 3.2, though with *DeleteFromTree* this is partially obscured by the amount of extra code needed for deletion.

The procedures *OnTree* and *InsertOnTree* are quite straightforward and need no explanation. We merely comment that they are more closely related to the equivalent sequences for unordered lists than those for ordered lists. This is due to the nature of the searching process. With ordered lists, the search may fail either because the list becomes exhausted (when the search key is greater than all numbers in the list) or because a larger item is found: for unordered lists and trees, these two situations coalesce into one.

The procedure *DeleteFromTree* is more difficult, the difficulty arising from the problem of deleting an internal node of the tree. There is no simple analogue of *Behead* for trees. Fig. 3.3 illustrates the cases which can arise while deleting various mnemonics from the second tree of Fig. 3.1, which is reproduced in this figure.

We consider these in turn:

(i) The item may be held at a leaf of the tree. An example in Fig. 3.3 is JOV. The node is returned to the heap and the pointer referring to it, here the *right* field of the node whose *item* is JNE, is set to **nil**.

(ii) The item may be held in a node whose left branch is null. An example is ADD in Fig. 3.3. The node is returned to the heap and the pointer referring to it, here the *left* field of the node whose *item* is LDA, is made to refer instead to its right branch, here the node whose *item* is DIV.

Fig. 3.3. Deleting items from a search tree.

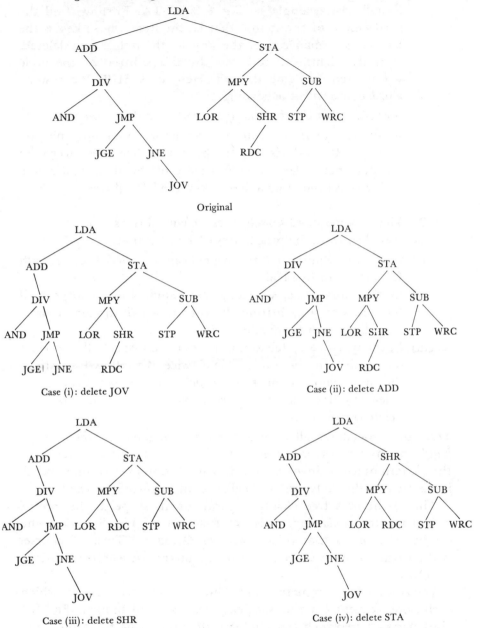

Original

Case (i): delete JOV

Case (ii): delete ADD

Case (iii): delete SHR

Case (iv): delete STA

Note that in Fig. 3.2 these two cases are combined.

(iii) The item may be held in a node whose right branch is null. An example in Fig. 3.3 is SHR. This is simply the mirror image of case (ii).

(iv) The item may be held in a node neither of whose branches is null. An example in Fig. 3.3 is STA. First we find the predecessor of the item – that is, the item whose key is the largest one smaller than the key of the item being deleted. It is the rightmost node on the left subtree of the node whose item is being deleted. Here it is SHR. We assume a procedure with the heading:

procedure *FindPredecessor* (var *pred* : *treeptr*; *t* : *treeptr*)

which sets *pred* to point to the node containing the predecessor. Its body is left to the reader. We then overwrite the item being deleted with a copy of this item, and delete (recursively) the original item from the left subtree.

3.2 The importance of search trees: balanced trees

It is clear from the procedures of Fig. 3.2 that:

(i) Insertion requires us to inspect all the nodes on a path from the root to a leaf.

(ii) In the worst case, searching also requires us to inspect all the nodes on a path from the root to a leaf, though in many cases the search terminates earlier.

(iii) In the worst case, deletion requires us to inspect all the nodes on a path from the root to a leaf twice. We follow the path to the node whose item is being deleted, we then proceed to a leaf to find the predecessor, and we repeat this path to delete the old node.

Thus the procedures all take a time proportional to the *average height* of the tree. What we mean by average, of course, depends on the pattern of access involved; but in what follows we assume that all items are equally likely, and will talk just of the *height* of the tree.

The height of a tree clearly depends on its shape. If the tree of n nodes is *well balanced*, as is the first tree of Fig. 3.1, then the height $\approx \log_2 n$ so that operations are $O(\log n)$. This, of course, is the virtue of using a tree rather than a linked list where operations are $O(n)$.

Unfortunately, completely unbalanced trees can arise in which each node (except for the one leaf) has one null branch. Fig. 3.4 gives parts of two such trees holding the mnemonic function codes of our computer.

Clearly the processing of such trees is $O(n)$, the same as that of processing linear lists. Worse, the constant of proportionality is greater, due to the test required to determine which branch to

Fig. 3.4. Two degenerate search trees.

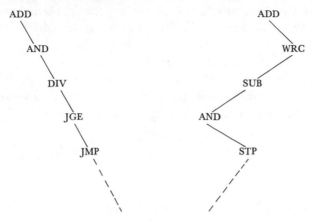

follow, and the tree requires more store for the second pointer. So this situation must be avoided! Trees must be kept as balanced as possible. Where the tree is only to be searched, as in a mnemonic function table, in practice, this poses no problem: the tree is initially created as balanced. Where there are to be continuous insertions and/or deletions, in a compiler symbol table for example, the problem is more difficult.

A great deal of work has been done in defining what constitutes balance and how to organise the tree so that the $O(\log n)$ characteristic is preserved during insertion and deletion. We will not pursue the matter here. The reader is referred to Wirth (1976) for discussion of height-balanced trees and 2–3 trees, for example.

Search trees can be trivially adapted to sorting. The items to be sorted are first added to a search tree and then written out in order by the *WriteTree* procedure shown in Fig. 3.5, which assumes the existence of the same procedure *WriteItem* as was used with *WriteList* in Fig. 2.2.

Fig. 3.5. Writing out a search tree in order.

```
procedure WriteTree(t:treeptr);
  begin
  if t <> nil then
    begin
    WriteTree(t↑.left);
    WriteItem(t↑.item);
    WriteTree(t↑.right)
    end
  end { of procedure "WriteTree" };
```

The *WriteTree* procedure capitalises on the key property of a search tree: the keys of all the items on the left subtree of any node are less than the key of the item at the node, which in turn is less than the keys of all the items on the right subtree.

Assuming that the tree can be kept balanced at each insertion, the combined procedure, called *TreeSort*, is quite efficient. Inserting an item on the tree takes a time proportional to the number of items currently on the tree. Thus to add all n items takes a time roughly proportional to:

$$\log(1) + \log(2) + \dots \log(n)$$
$$= \log(1 \times 2 \times \dots n)$$
$$= \log(n!)$$

which, given Stirling's approximation of $n!$, is $O(n \log n)$. The actual writing takes a time proportional to the number of items, n, so that the time for *TreeSort* is $O(n \log n)$.

This is much better than the simple sorting methods, such as the linear selection sort or bubble sort, which are $O(n^2)$. However it is not often used in sorting applications because of the space required to hold the pointers.

We return to better sorting methods in Chapter 4.

3.3   Preorder, inorder and postorder procedures

The *WriteTree* procedure given above is an example of *binary recursion*: that is, each invocation of *WriteTree* involves two further invocations. The searching, inserting and deleting procedures, it should be noted, involve only linear recursion: although there are two (or more) written recursive calls only one of them is obeyed on each invocation.

In *WriteTree* the processing of the node is done between the recursive calls. Accordingly we refer to this as an *inorder* procedure. We expand the notion of *preorder* (where the processing is done before the recursive call) and *postorder* (where it is done after) to include binary as well as linear recursion. Fig. 3.6 gives the classical schemata for these procedures, using the same conventions as those of Fig. 2.20.

Fig. 3.6. Schemata for preorder, inorder and postorder procedures.

```
procedure PreOrder(x:xtype);
  begin
  if P(x) then M(x)
  else
```

```
          begin
          S1(x);
          PreOrder(F1(x));
          PreOrder(F2(x));
          end
      end { of procedure "PreOrder" };

    procedure InOrder(x:xtype);
      begin
      if P(x) then M(x)
      else
        begin
        InOrder(F1(x));
        S2(x);
        InOrder(F2(x))
        end
      end { of procedure "InOrder" };

    procedure PostOrder(x:xtype);
      begin
      if P(x) then M(x)
      else
        begin
        PostOrder(F1(x));
        PostOrder(F2(x));
        S3(x)
        end
      end { of procedure "PostOrder" };
```

Note that *WriteTree* conforms to the inorder schema though we have replaced:

by:
if $t =$ nil then { *do nothing* }
else
if $t <>$ nil then

3.4 Some general binary recursive tree processing procedures

It is with binary recursion that the naturalness spoken of in Chapter 1 becomes apparent. In Fig. 3.7 we give a procedure for copying a tree.

Fig. 3.7. A procedure for copying a tree.
```
procedure CopyTree(var t1:treeptr; t2:treeptr);
  begin
  if t2 = nil then t1 := nil
  else
    begin
    new(t1);
    t1↑.item := t2↑.item;
    CopyTree(t1↑.left,t2↑.left);
    CopyTree(t1↑.right,t2↑.right)
    end
  end { of procedure "CopyTree" };
```

It is clearly a preorder procedure.

The reader will recognise, probably without having to turn back to the appropriate page, that this procedure is almost the same as that given for copying a list in Fig. 2.3: the differences in the procedures reflect the differences in the data structures involved.

By contrast, Fig. 3.8 gives a non-recursive procedure. Not only is it difficult to understand and write, but it bears precious little relationship to the corresponding procedure for lists given in Fig. 2.6.

Fig. 3.8. A non-recursive procedure for copying a tree.

```
procedure CopyTree(var t1:treeptr; t2:treeptr);
  var branch:(l,r);
      temp,p:treeptr;
      s:stack of <treeptr,treeptr>;
  begin
  clear s;
  new(t1);
  push <t1,t2> onto s;
  repeat
    pop <p,t2> from s;
    branch := r;
    while t2 <> nil do
      begin
      new(temp);
      if branch = l then p↑.left := temp else p↑.right := temp;
      temp↑.item := t2↑.item;
      push <temp,t2↑.right> onto s;
      p := temp; branch := l; t2 := t2↑.left
      end;
    if branch = l then p↑.left := nil else p↑.right := nil
  until s empty;
  temp := t1; t1 := t1↑.right;
  dispose(temp)
  end { of procedure "CopyTree" };
```

As all non-recursive versions of binary recursive procedures require a stack or its equivalent, we will take the appropriateness of recursive procedures for granted for the rest of the book: no further non-recursive versions will be given until Chapter 8 where we discuss the elimination of recursion more fully.

As a final example we give, in Fig. 3.9, a postorder procedure for disposing of trees.

Fig. 3.9. A procedure for disposing of trees.

```
procedure DisposeTree(t:treeptr);
  begin
  if t <> nil then
```

```
        begin
          DisposeTree(t↑.left);
          DisposeTree(t↑.right);
          dispose(t)
        end
    end { of procedure "DisposeTree" };
```

All these procedures visit each node once and once only, so that they are $O(n)$ where n is the number of nodes.

3.5   Expression trees

We turn now to a second specific application of binary trees, *expression trees*. These arise in compilers, interpreters, theorem provers, indeed in any application in which arithmetic or Boolean expressions are processed. In Fig. 3.10 we give two such trees - for the expressions:

$$b^2-4ac \quad \text{and} \quad h(e+4f+g)/3$$

Fig. 3.10. Two expression trees.

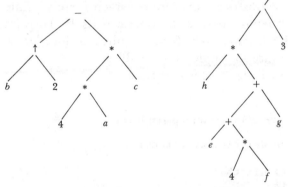

The salient feature of the expression tree is that the item of each internal node is an operator and its branches point to each of its operands. In the first tree of Fig. 3.10 the operands of − are $b↑2$ and $4*a*c$; the operands of ↑ are b and 2, and so on. The leaves contain either variables or constants. We consider how such a tree may be created from a string of characters in Chapter 5.†

In some applications the items at the leaves will simply be characters, in others they will contain more information. For the next two sections we assume the definition:

   type *itemtype* $= char$

---

† The procedure *Expression* of Fig. 5.6 does not handle exponentiation, but it is a trivial matter to extend it.

Note that this implies that any constant in an expression will be less than 10. We also assume that all operators are binary.

3.6   Writing expression trees

It is a trivial matter to write out the Reverse Polish form of any expression held in an expression tree as Fig. 3.11 shows.

Fig. 3.11. Printing a tree in Reverse Polish form.

```
procedure WriteRP(t:treeptr);
  begin
  if t <> nil then
    begin
    WriteRP(t↑.left);
    WriteRP(t↑.right);
    write(t↑.item)
    end
  end { of procedure "WriteRP" };
```

This is a simple postorder procedure which merely prints the two operands of an operator before the operator itself. To print out the expression in the normal *infix* form requires an inorder procedure, though it is not quite so simple as we shall see.

The procedure of Fig. 3.12 is inadequate.

Fig. 3.12. *WriteInfix* with no parentheses.

```
procedure WriteInfix(t:treeptr);
  begin
  if t <> nil then
    begin
    WriteInfix(t↑.left);
    write(t↑.item);
    WriteInfix(t↑.right)
    end
  end { of procedure "WriteInfix" };
```

For the second example of Fig. 3.10 it produces:

$$h*e+4*f+g/3$$

instead of:

$$h*(e+4*f+g)/3$$

Clearly we need to print parentheses to overcome the normal priority of operators.

An extreme solution is given in Fig. 3.13.

56

Fig. 3.13. *WriteInfix* with a surfeit of parentheses.

```
procedure WriteInfix(t:treeptr);
  begin
  if t <> nil then
    begin
    write('(');
    WriteInfix(t↑.left);
    write(t↑.item);
    WriteInfix(t↑.right);
    write(')')
    end
  end { of procedure "WriteInfix" };
```

It uses parentheses to indicate explicitly the priority of all operators. For the example used above it produces:

$$(((h)*(((e)+((4)*(f)))+(g)))/(3))$$

which is correct but unreadably redundant. What we require is a procedure that inserts precisely the right number of parentheses.

First we notice that if an operand is a variable or a constant then it needs no parentheses. Thus the *WriteInfix* procedure must take as its special case not the null tree as has been the case so far but a leaf, since the items at the leaves are variables and constants.

The items of the internal nodes are operators and for each of these we need to determine whether its left operand and independently its right operand requires parentheses.

If we assume the existence of two Boolean functions *LeftParentheses* and *RightParentheses* which determine whether parentheses are required and a variable *operand* of type **set of** *char* which has the constant value $['a' .. 'z', '0' .. '9']$ then the procedure of Fig. 3.14 operates correctly.

Fig. 3.14. *WriteInfix* with just the right number of parentheses.

```
procedure WriteInfix(t:treeptr);
  begin
  if t↑.item in operand then
    write(t↑.item)
  else
    begin
    { First write the left operand }
    if LeftParentheses then
      begin
      write('('); WriteInfix(t↑.left); write(')')
      end
    else
      WriteInfix(t↑.left);
    { Then write the operator }
```

```
        write(t↑.item);
        { Finally write the right operand }
        if RightParentheses then
          begin
          write('('); WriteInfix(t↑.right); write(')')
          end
        else
          WriteInfix(t↑.right)
        end
    end { of procedure "WriteInfix" };
```

Before we proceed we should point out that the procedures we give are now becoming less trivial so that there are many different ways of expressing them. We will choose to concentrate on making them as clear as possible, even if it means that the procedures are not as fast or as small as they could be. If our idea of clarity does not correspond with that of the reader we offer our apologies.

Note that the recursion does not terminate in Fig. 3.12 when t is the null tree: it terminates one level above, where t is a leaf. This illustrates an important difference between search trees and expression trees. In search trees all the nodes contain items of the same type; in expression trees there are two classes: leaves holding operands and internal nodes holding operators. Clearly all procedures processing expression trees will differentiate between the two. Here we have

Fig. 3.15. Some examples appropriate to *LeftParentheses*.

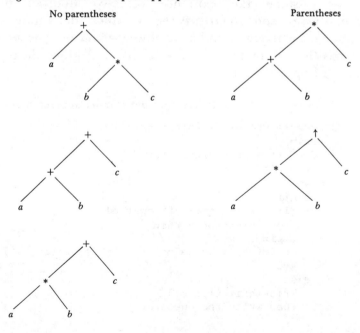

58

differentiated by testing the item. Of course, we could have tested for a leaf by testing whether its branches were null. This, however, seems a little obtuse and we will always use the more direct method.

Returning to the infix printing procedure, the key to *WriteInfix*, of course, lies in the procedures *LeftParentheses* and *RightParentheses*. In order to determine whether or not parentheses are required it is perhaps best to draw out trees which illustrate the cases that can occur. Fig. 3.15 is appropriate to *LeftParentheses*. The three trees to the left do not require parentheses, the two to the right do.

While these examples are not exhaustive, they are sufficiently representative for the rule to be deduced: only if the left branch points to an internal node whose operator is of a lower priority are parentheses needed. Assuming a function *Priority* which has as its value the priority of the operator which is its parameter, this rule can be expressed as shown in Fig. 3.16.

Fig. 3.16. The function *LeftParentheses*.

```
function LeftParentheses:Boolean;
  begin
  if t↑.left↑.item in operand then
    LeftParentheses := false
  else
    LeftParentheses := Priority(t↑.item) > Priority(t↑.left↑.item)
  end { of function "LeftParentheses" };
```

The function *RightParentheses* is a little more complicated because of the left associativity rule for operators. Consider the first example of Fig. 3.17.

Fig. 3.17. Two examples peculiar to *RightParentheses*.

Clearly brackets are required because the tree represents $a - (b - c)$ which is quite different from $a - b - c$. Thus the rule must be extended to insert parentheses where the operator at the node on the right branch has the same priority as that at the parent node.

But what about the second tree of Fig. 3.17? The expressions $a + (b + c)$ and $a + b + c$ are equivalent but which should we write? It very much depends on the application. If the tree was produced directly from input, and if we wished to print it out in as close a form to the original as possible we would leave the brackets in, since they must have been there originally to have produced that tree. If, however, the tree had been produced by substitution operations, or if we wished to write out the 'simplest' form, we would omit them. We have chosen this latter solution in Fig. 3.18.

Fig. 3.18. The function *RightParentheses*.

```
function RightParentheses:Boolean;
  begin
  if t↑.right↑.item in operand then
    RightParentheses := false
  else if t↑.item in ['+','*'] then
    RightParentheses := Priority(t↑.item) > Priority(t↑.right↑.i
  else
    RightParentheses := Priority(t↑.item) >= Priority(t↑.right↑.
  end { of function "RightParentheses" };
```

3.7 An example: symbolic differentiation

In the introductory paragraphs to this book we mentioned, as an illustration of recursion at work, a procedure which will differentiate with respect to x an expression held in an expression tree. We return to it now. For brevity, we restrict the operators to + and *. The formulae for differentiation are well known. If u and v are subexpressions then:

$$\frac{d}{dx}(u+v) = \frac{du}{dx} + \frac{dv}{dx}$$

$$\frac{d}{dx}(u*v) = u\frac{dv}{dx} + v\frac{du}{dx}$$

$$\frac{dx}{dx} = 1$$

$$\frac{dk}{dx} = 0 \quad \text{where } k \text{ is any constant or variable other than } x.$$

In Fig. 3.19 we give a procedure which directly implements these rules and produces a new tree $t1$ which is the differential of the tree $t2$. It uses the procedure *CopyTree* of Fig. 3.7.

Fig. 3.19. A symbolic differentiation procedure.

```
procedure Diff(var t1:treeptr; t2:treeptr);
  var u,v,du,dv,udv,vdu:treeptr;
  begin
  if t2↑.item = '+' then
    { d(u+v)/dx = du/dx+dv/dx }
```

60

```
            begin
            Diff(du,t2↑.left); Diff(dv,t2↑.right);
            NewTree(tl,du,'+',dv)
            end
         else if t2↑.item = '*' then
            { d(u*v)/dx = u(dv/dx)+v(du/dx) }
            begin
            CopyTree(u,t2↑.left); Diff(dv,t2↑.right);
            NewTree(udv,u,'*',dv);
            CopyTree(v,t2↑.right); Diff(du,t2↑.left);
            NewTree(vdu,v,'*',du);
            NewTree(tl,udv,'+',vdu)
            end
         else if t2↑.item = 'x' then
            { dx/dx = 1 }
            NewTree(tl,nil,'1',nil)
         else
            NewTree(tl,nil,'0',nil)
         end { of procedure "Diff" };
```

The tree produced by *Diff* is clearly quite large. Given the expression x^2+5x mentioned in the introduction (which we have of course to rephrase as $xx+5x$ because of the limitations of *Diff*) it produces the tree of Fig. 3.20.

Fig. 3.20. The tree produced by *Diff* for $xx + 5x$.

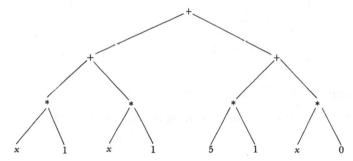

We can simplify this substantially by using the normal identities of arithmetic:

$$x+0 = x = 0+x$$
$$x*1 = x = 1*x$$
$$x*0 = 0 = 0*x$$

and we now consider a procedure to do this. We must effectively work from the bottom up. If a node contains a variable or constant then it is a leaf and is as simple as possible. If it is an internal node then we may be able to apply the identities. This is true if one or other of its branches points to a leaf either originally or as a result of the simplification of its subtrees.

A procedure is given in Fig. 3.21 which simplifies the tree itself (as distinct from creating a new one) and returns unwanted nodes to the heap, using *DisposeTree* of Fig. 3.9.

Fig. 3.21. A procedure for simplifying a tree.

```
procedure Simplify(var t:treeptr);
    var temp:treeptr;
    begin
    if t↑.item in operand then { do nothing }
    else
       begin
       Simplify(t↑.left); Simplify(t↑.right);
       if (t↑.item = '+') and (t↑.right↑.item = '0')
       or (t↑.item = '*') and (t↑.right↑.item = '1')
       or (t↑.item = '*') and (t↑.left↑.item = '0') then
          { x+0=x, x*1=x, 0*x=0 }
          begin
          temp := t; t:= t↑.left; temp↑.left := nil;
          DisposeTree(temp)
          end
       else if (t↑.item = '+') and (t↑.left↑.item = '0')
       or (t↑.item = '*') and (t↑.left↑.item = '1')
       or (t↑.item = '*') and (t↑.right↑.item = '0') then
          { 0+x=x, 1*x=x, x*0=0 }
          begin
          temp := t; t := t↑.right; temp↑.right := nil;
          DisposeTree(temp)
          end
       { else do nothing }
       end
    end { of procedure "Simplify" };
```

The result of simplifying the tree of Fig. 3.20 is given in Fig. 3.22.

Fig. 3.22. The result of simplifying the tree of Fig. 3.20.

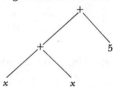

This particular tree suggests other operations we might wish to apply to expression trees such as replacing the subtree representing *x+x* by one representing *2*x*. In any system for manipulating expressions we would wish to perform many such operations. Further we would wish to perform arithmetic so that a subtree representing 2+5 could be reduced to 7. We leave such explorations to the reader as part of one of the exercises at the end of the chapter.

3.8   Another example: evaluating an expression

Often it is useful to make the item at a node richer in information. Suppose that, in an interpreter say, we wish to find the value of an expression held as a tree given the value of the variables which are its operands. In terms of one of the examples given earlier we want the value of b^2-4ac given the values of a, b and c. It would be possible to produce a procedure for this which operated on a tree in which the items at the nodes were characters. It is much more reasonable to have a more general tree in which:

(i) a constant is represented by its value;
(ii) a variable is represented by the index, of type *range*, in the array *data* in which its value is held;
(iii) an operator is represented by an enumerated type.

If we consider unary as well as binary operators, and assume that our expressions are real rather than integer then an appropriate definition might be:

> **type** *tagtype* = (*constant, variable, unary, binary*);
>   *itemtype* = **record**
>   **case** *tag* : *tagtype* **of**
>   *constant* : (*value* : *real*);
>   *variable* : (*index* : *range*);
>   *unary* : (*unop* : (*neg*));
>   *binary* : (*binop* : (*add, sub, mult, dvd, expon*))
>   **end**

Note that this definition introduces the type *unop* which has only one value *neg*. This is to allow for the inclusion of further unary operators later. However we can go further. As we have noted before nodes are of two types: internal nodes and leaves. An internal node has an operator as its item and a leaf has an operand. In both cases the node is provided with two branches even though, by definition, both are null when the node is an operand, and one is when the node is a unary operator. Since we are already differentiating the nodes by the tag, it makes sense to extend the differentiation to eliminate these null branches. The type *itemtype* becomes redundant and *node* which has been defined so far as:

> **type** *node* = **record**
>   *left* : *treeptr*;
>   *item* : *itemtype*;
>   *right* : *treeptr*
>   **end**

becomes instead:

```
type node = record
              case tag : tagtype of
              constant : (value : real);
              variable : (index : range);
              unary : (unop : (neg);
                       branch : treeptr);
              binary : (left : treeptr :
                       binop : (add, sub, mult, dvd, expon);
                       right : treeptr)
              end
```

A function for evaluating an expression held in such a tree is given in Fig. 3.23 in which a function *Power*, closely related to the functions of Chapter 1, is assumed.

Fig. 3.23. A function for evaluating an expression.

```
function ExprValue(t:treeptr):real;
  var v1,v2:real;
  begin
  case t↑.tag of
  constant:
    ExprValue := t↑.value;
  variable:
    ExprValue := data[t↑.index];
  unary:
    begin
    v1 := ExprValue(t↑.branch);
    case t↑.unop of
    neg: ExprValue := -v1
    end { of cases on "t↑.unop" }
    end { of case "unary" };
  binary:
    begin
    v1 := ExprValue(t↑.left);
    v2 := ExprValue(t↑.right);
    case t↑.binop of
    add:ExprValue := v1+v2;
    sub:ExprValue := v1-v2;
    mult:ExprValue := v1*v2;
    dvd:ExprValue := v1/v2;
    expon:ExprValue := Power(v1,v2)
    end { of cases on "t↑.binop" }
    end { of case "binary" }
  end { of cases on "t↑.tag" }
  end { of function "ExprValue" };
```

3.9 Binary decision trees

As a third and final illustration of binary trees we consider *decision trees*.

Our particular example will be related to *Huffman codes*. In contrast to codes like ASCII, which are of fixed length, Huffman codes have variable length. The more frequently used characters have short codes and the less frequently used ones have longer codes. This means that, on average, a message will require fewer bits than for fixed length codes.

Let us use a hypothetical example in which there are six characters coded:

α	0
β	1110
γ	100
δ	1111
ε	110
ζ	101

The relationship between these codes can be expressed quite clearly in diagrammatical form as shown in Fig. 3.24.

Fig. 3.24. A binary tree representing Huffman codes.

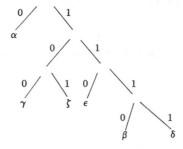

Clearly the labels on the branches are redundant since all left branches are labelled 0, and all right branches, 1. Note that there is no information stored at internal nodes, so that an appropriate definition of a node is:

```
type tagtype = (internal, leaf);
     node = record
              case tag : tagtype of
              internal : (left, right : treeptr);
              leaf : (ch : char)
            end
```

We need to be able:

(i) to create the appropriate tree for a given character set;
(ii) to produce a list of codes from a given tree;
(iii) to decode a string of characters coded in a given code.

We leave (i) and (ii) as exercises, and give in Fig. 3.25 a procedure which decodes the next character held on a file of type *binaryfile* defined:

type *binaryfile* = **file of** 0..1

Fig. 3.25. A procedure for decoding a Huffman code.

```
procedure Decode(var f:binaryfile; t:treeptr; var ch:char);

  procedure D(t:treeptr);
    begin
    if t↑.tag = leaf then ch := t↑.ch
    else if f↑ = 0 then
      begin
      get(f);
      D(t↑.left)
      end
    else { if f↑ = 1 then }
      begin
      get(f);
      D(t↑.right)
      end
    end { of procedure "D" };

  begin
  D(t)
  end { of procedure "Decode" };
```

EXERCISES

3.1 Write a function with the heading:
function *Height*(*t* : *treeptr*) : *natural*
whose value is the height of the tree (pointed to by) *t*. Assume that a null tree has a height of 0.

3.2 Write a function with the heading:
function *NoNodes*(*t* : *treeptr*) : *natural*
whose value is the number of nodes on the tree *t*.

3.3 Write a function with the heading:
function *Equal*(*t*1, *t*2 : *treeptr*) : *Boolean*
which has the value *true* if *t*1 and *t*2 have the same structure and the same item at each node.

3.4 The notion of a *balanced tree* can be formalised by defining a tree to be balanced if and only if the number of nodes on the left subtree of every node differs by at most one from the number of nodes on the right subtree. Write a function with the heading:

function *Balanced(t : treeptr) : Boolean*

which has the value *true* if the tree *t* is balanced, and *false* otherwise.

3.5 Write a Pascal program cross-referencer which will produce, for a given Pascal program, a list in alphabetical order, of all the identifiers used. Each identifier should be followed by a list, in numerical order, of the lines in which the identifier appeared. (From Wirth (1976).)

Use a binary search tree to hold the identifiers and a linked-linear list for the line numbers associated with each identifier.

3.6 Write a procedure that will evaluate a logical formula such as the one shown in Fig. 3.26.

Fig. 3.26. A Boolean expression tree.

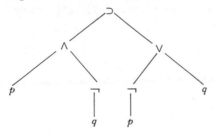

The variables have values *true* and *false* (as for Pascal's Booleans); there is a unary operation ¬ (not) with the obvious interpretation; and four binary operators ∧ (and), ∨ (or), ⊃ (implies) and ≡ (equivalent to) whose operations are defined in the table of Fig. 3.27 in which x and y are assumed to be the two arguments.

Fig. 3.27 The definition of the logical operators.

x	y	$x \wedge y$	$x \vee y$	$x \supset y$	$x \equiv y$
false	false	false	false	true	true
false	true	false	true	true	false
true	false	false	true	false	false
true	true	true	true	true	true

3.7 Write a more complete symbolic differentiation procedure than that of §3.7 which will deal with expressions containing real constants and the usual logarithmic and trigonometrical functions (which you can regard as unary operators) as well as the arithmetic operators. The form of tree should be that of §3.8.

3.8 Write a general procedure for simplifying expressions held as a tree such as that of Ex. 3.7. Use it to simplify the results of the differentiation.

3.9 The Huffman codes for a set of characters can be produced in tree form, assuming that the relative frequencies of the characters are known, as follows:

The two characters with the lowest frequencies are chosen and a subtree created with them at the leaves. A pseudo-character is created with a frequency equal to the sum of the frequencies of the characters just chosen; and the process repeated with the remaining characters augmented by this new pseudo-character. Thus the tree grows from the bottom.

The tree of Fig. 3.24 has been produced in this way from the table of frequencies:

α	0.45
β	0.07
γ	0.12
δ	0.08
ϵ	0.15
ζ	0.13

Write a procedure to create a Huffman tree for a given character set.

3.10 Write a procedure that will produce a list of codes from the information contained in a Huffman tree.

4

Binary recursion without trees

Although binary recursion is most often associated with binary trees, it is nevertheless relevant in many situations where there are no trees, including the fundamentally important one of sorting. We consider some of these in this chapter. The characteristic of such a problem is that its solution can be expressed in terms of the solution of two subproblems of the same type.

4.1 An illustration: Towers of Hanoi

The classical illustrative example is provided by the Towers of Hanoi. Legends abound about these towers, but essentially they consist of three vertical pegs, on one of which is initially placed a tower of n rings of different diameters, each ring resting on one of a larger diameter.

Fig. 4.1 shows a simple example with a tower of three rings on the first rod.

Fig. 4.1. The Towers of Hanoi.

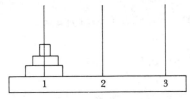

The problem is to move the tower to a second peg, using the third as a temporary resting place, subject to the constraints:

(i) only one ring may be moved at a time;
(ii) no ring may ever rest on one of a smaller diameter.

The solution to the problem is expressed very elegantly in a recursive form:

(i) If we can move a tower of k rings from one peg to another we can certainly move a tower of $k+1$ rings by:

    (a) moving the top k rings to the third peg;

    (b) moving the bottom ring directly to the second peg;

    (c) moving the tower of k rings from the third back to the second.

(ii) We can trivially move a tower of one ring.

Thus we can move a tower of n rings for any (positive) value of n. Fig. 4.2 illustrates this with respect to the tower of Fig. 4.1.

Fig. 4.2. Moving a tower of three rings.

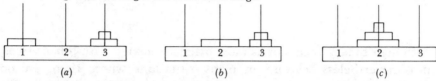

      (a)   (b)   (c)

The solution of a tower of three rings is as shown in Fig. 4.3.

Fig. 4.3 The solution for $n = 3$.

Move 1 to 2 ⎫
Move 1 to 3 ⎬ These move two rings from peg 1 to peg 3 to produce
Move 2 to 3 ⎭ state (a) of Fig. 4.2.
Move 1 to 2   State (b).
Move 3 to 1 ⎫
Move 3 to 2 ⎬ These move two rings from peg 3 back to peg 2 to
Move 1 to 2 ⎭ produce state (c).

A procedure producing such a solution follows immediately. It is shown in Fig. 4.4, in which we arbitrarily assume that the rings are to be moved from peg 1 to peg 2.

Fig. 4.4. A procedure for the Towers of Hanoi.

```
procedure Hanoi(n:natural);
  type pegtype = 1..3;

  procedure H(k:natural; p1,p2,p3:pegtype);
    begin
    if k = 1 then
      writeln(' Move ',p1:1,' to ',p2:1)
    else
      begin
      H(k-1,p1,p3,p2);
      writeln(' Move ',p1:1,' to ',p2:1);
      H(k-1,p3,p2,p1)
      end
    end { of procedure "H" };

  begin
  H(n,1,2,3)
  end { of procedure "Hanoi" };
```

70

4.2 Analysis of *Hanoi*

With trees our analyses were informal ones, and generally related time to the number of nodes on the tree or the average height of a tree. With the Towers of Hanoi procedure there is no explicit tree, but we can instead do a formal analysis using a recurrence relation.

As in Chapter 1, T_k is the number of operations required to solve a problem of size k. Here the explicitly defined case arises where $k=1$. Thus we have the relation:

$$T_k = b + 2T_{k-1}, \quad k \neq 1$$
$$= a, \qquad\qquad k=1$$

where a represents a test $(k=1)$ and the operations involved in the writing, and b represents a test $(k=1)$, the operations involved in the writing and two procedure calls, each of which involves, as well as the actual call, a subtraction $(k-1)$ and the assignment of four parameters.

We solve the recurrence relation by substitution:

$$\begin{aligned}
T_n &= b + 2T_{n-1} \\
&= b + 2(b+2T_{n-2}) \\
&= b + 2b + 2^2 T_{n-2} \\
&= b + 2b + 2^2(b+2T_{n-3}) \\
&= (1+2+2^2)b + 2^3 T_{n-3}
\end{aligned}$$

$$\vdots$$

$$\begin{aligned}
&= (1+2+2^2+\ldots 2^{n-2})b + 2^{n-1}T_1 \\
&= (1+2+2^2+\ldots 2^{n-2})b + 2^{n-1}a \\
&= (2^{n-1}-1)b + 2^{n-1}a \\
&= 2^{n-1}(a+b) - b
\end{aligned}$$

Let us use this formula to count the number of elementary operations. For a we have $1+M$, where M is the number of operations involved in writing; for b we have 1 (for the test) $+ M$ (for writing) $+ 10$ (for 2 calls) $+ 2$ (for 2 subtractions) $+ 8$ (for the parameters): a total of $21+M$. Thus

$$\begin{aligned}
T_n &= 2^{n-1}(1+M+21+M)-(21+M) \\
&= 2^{n-1}(22+2M)-21-M \\
&= 2^n(11+M)-21-M
\end{aligned}$$

There are precisely 2^n-1 moves so we see that the overheads of the procedure are approximately 11 elementary operations per move.

4.3 Verifying the solution of recurrence relations

So far whenever we have had a recurrence relation we have solved it by substitution, or where it has been closely related to an earlier one, we have left it for the reader to do at his leisure. However, this substitution technique depends on recognising the correct pattern, and is therefore fallible. We consider now a method of *proving* our solutions: the method of *induction*.

We illustrate this with respect to the last example. That is we prove that if:

$$T_k = b + 2T_{k-1}, \quad k \neq 1$$
$$\quad = a, \qquad\qquad k = 1$$

then:

$$T_n = 2^{n-1}(a+b) - b$$

The proof has two parts:

(i) First we prove it is true for the explicitly specified case:

$$T_1 = 2^{1-1}(a+b) - b$$
$$\quad = (a+b) - b$$
$$\quad = a$$

(ii) Then assuming it is true for size $k-1$ (and in general for sizes $k-2, k-3, \ldots$) we prove it is true for size k:

$$T_n = b + 2T_{n-1}$$
$$\quad = b + 2[2^{n-2}(a+b) - b]$$
$$\quad = b + 2[2^{n-2}(a+b)] - 2b$$
$$\quad = 2^{n-1}(a+b) - b$$

In what follows we may present a proof rather than a derivation (or leave the proof to the reader) if this enhances the text.

4.4 A variation on *Hanoi*

Let us see now how the solution to a recurrence relation enables us to determine the effects of changes to the procedure.

Let us consider the effect of stopping the recursion one step later: that is of explicitly defining how to move 0 rings instead of 1. This is, of course, trivial and Fig. 4.5 gives an appropriate procedure.

Fig. 4.5. Another procedure for the Towers of Hanoi.

```
procedure Hanoi(n:natural);
   type pegtype = 1..3;

   procedure H(k:natural; p1,p2,p3:pegtype);
```

```
      begin
      if k = 0 then { do nothing }
      else
         begin
         H(k-1,p1,p3,p2);
         writeln(' Move ',p1:1,' to ',p2:1);
         H(k-1,p3,p2,p1)
         end
      end { of procedure "H" };

   begin
   H(n,1,2,3)
   end { of procedure "Hanoi" };
```

If the number of operations are now called a' and b' then the recurrence relation is:

$$T_k' = b' + 2T_{k-1}', \quad k \neq 0$$
$$= a', \qquad\qquad k=0$$

whose solution is:

$$T_n' = 2^n(a'+b') - b'$$

as compared with the original:

$$T_n = 2^{n-1}(a+b) - b$$

In terms of elementary operations, a' is simply 1, and b' is the same as b, that is $21+M$. Substituting we get:

$$T_n' = 2^n(22+M) - 21 - M$$

as compared with:

$$T_n = 2^n(11+M) - 21 - M$$

As the cost of M approaches 0 the ratio T_n'/T_n approaches 2, and as M approaches ∞, it approaches 1. Thus we see that the choice of where to stop the recursion can significantly affect the performance. Compare this with the case of linear recursion, where the differences are generally negligible.

Other changes such as replacing the write-statement by $H(1, p1, p2, p3)$ in the general sequence of Fig. 4.4 are left as exercises.

4.5   Trees of procedure calls

While there is no explicit concept of a tree in the Towers of Hanoi, there is nevertheless an implicit tree involved which it is quite instructive to consider. It is the *tree of procedure calls* of Fig. 4.6. This shows via the full lines how a given invocation of *H* causes further invocations until, at the bottom, the recursion terminates. The root of the tree corresponds to *Hanoi* which invokes *H* initially. (We have also included, via the dotted lines, the moves

that the invocations generate, using '→' as an abbreviation of 'Move
. . . to'.)

Fig. 4.6. The tree of procedure calls for Towers of Hanoi.

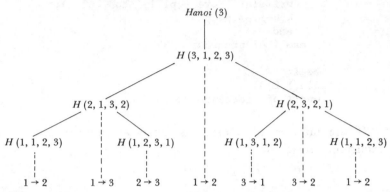

We can see that for *Hanoi*(n) the tree has $2^n - 1$ nodes, so that the
procedure is linear in the number of nodes but exponential in n.
Where the solution of the recurrence relations proves difficult, as
in a later chapter, we will find these trees very useful in analysing
procedures.

4.6 Adaptive integration

The Towers of Hanoi is simply an amusement. We pass now
to the more serious matter of *adaptive integration*.

Let us suppose we have a procedure with the following heading:

procedure *Int*(**function** $f(x:real):real; a,b:real;$

var *approx,eps:real*)

which sets *approx* to an approximation to $\int_a^b f(x)\ \mathrm{d}x$ and *eps* to an
estimate of its accuracy; and that we require a function which will
calculate the integral to a specified accuracy, e. Its heading could be:

function *Integral*(**function** $f(x:real):real; a,b,e:real):real$

Simply calling *Int* will not do, because it may not give the required
accuracy. However, it is well known that the smaller the interval of
integration the better the accuracy. Thus, if *Int* does not give the
required accuracy, we simply split the interval (a, b) into two halves,
and integrate each half separately. An appropriate procedure is
given in Fig. 4.7 in which, ignoring the numerical analysis involved,
we have asked for an accuracy of $e/2$ for each half interval.

It is important to note how *Integral* adapts to the function f being
integrated. Since each half of the interval is integrated independently

Fig. 4.7. An adaptive integration function.

```
function Integral(function f(x:real):real; a,b,e:real):real;
  var approx,eps:real;
  begin
  Int(f,a,b,approx,eps);
  if abs(eps) <= abs(e) then
    Integral := approx
  else
    Integral := Integral(f,a,(a+b)/2,e/2)
               + Integral(f,(a+b)/2,b,e/2)
  end { of function "Integral" };
```

it may happen that one of the intervals needs to be further halved while the other does not.

4.7 A sorting procedure: *MergeSort*

Sorting, a subject we touched upon in the last chapter, is a fundamental operation in data processing so that it is important to have procedures that work as fast as possible. Let us assume definitions:

type *sizetype* = 0..*max*;
    itemtype = record
                key:*keytype*;
                info:*infotype*
                end;
    seqtype = array [*sizetype*] of *itemtype*

where *max* is an appropriate constant and *keytype* and *infotype* are left unspecified.

As is well known the simple sorting procedures such as *linear selection* and *bubble sort* are $O(n^2)$, where *n* is the number of items to be sorted. We will take a small diversion to consider one of these, *linear selection*, to set the scene for the more efficient *MergeSort* to be introduced presently. Fig. 4.8 gives a (linear recur-

Fig. 4.8. A procedure for sorting by linear selection.

```
procedure SelectionSort(var seq:seqtype; n:sizetype);
  var s:sizetype;
      temp:itemtype;
  begin
  if n <> 1 then
    begin
    s := MaxIndex(seq,n);
    temp := seq[s]; seq[s] := seq[n]; seq[n] := temp;
    SelectionSort(seq,n-1)
    end
  end { of procedure "SelectionSort" };
```

sive) procedure, *SelectionSort*, in which the operation of finding the index of the largest element of *seq* is unspecified.

We can show that this is $O(n^2)$ quite simply. Since finding the largest element of a sequence of length n involves a constant part and a part proportional to k we have, for *SelectionSort* itself:

$$T_k = b + ck + T_{k-1}, \quad k \neq 1$$
$$= a, \qquad\qquad k = 1$$

whose solution:

$$T_n = \tfrac{1}{2}cn^2 + (b + \tfrac{1}{2}c)n + (a - b - c)$$

is easily established by substitution or proved by induction.

Note that *SelectionSort* has linear recursion and expresses the sorting of a sequence of length n in terms of sorting a sequence of length $n-1$.

MergeSort, which we now consider, expresses the sorting of a sequence of length n in terms of sorting two subsequences each of length $n/2$ and so exhibits binary recursion. The procedure merges two sorted subsequences to produce a sorted sequence which is, of course, why it is called *MergeSort*. It is not possible to merge two sequences *in situ*, and so we need a second array. Suppose we call the arrays x and y. Then *MergeSort* operates as follows: to get a sorted sequence into x, we first produce two sorted half-length subsequences in y and then merge them into x; to get each sorted subsequence in y, we first produce two sorted quarter-length subsequences in x and then merge them into y. Ultimately we need to get sorted subsequences of one element in either x or y depending on n. If the unsorted items are in x it is simplest to copy them initially into y. Fig. 4.9 gives a procedure in which, for the moment, the *Merge* procedure is left unspecified: it merges the sorted subsequences in $y_l \rightarrow y_{mid}$ and $y_{mid+1} \rightarrow y_u$ to produce a sorted sequence in $x_l \rightarrow x_u$. Ignore, for the moment, the values in the comments.

Fig. 4.9. A procedure for *MergeSort*.

```
procedure MergeSort(var seq:seqtype; n:sizetype);
  var seq1:seqtype;

  procedure M(var x,y:seqtype; l,u:sizetype);
    var mid:sizetype;
    begin
    if u = 1 then { do nothing }              { a=1, b=1 }
    else
      begin
      mid := (l+u) div 2;                     { b=3 }
      M(y,x,l,mid);                           { b=9 }
```

76

```
        M(y,x,mid+1,u);                        { b=10 }
        Merge(x,y,1,mid,u)                     { See Fig.4.11 }
      end
    end { of procedure "M" };

  begin
  seq1 := seq;
  M(seq,seq1,1,n)
  end { of procedure "Mergesort" };
```

Fig. 4.10 shows the tree of procedure calls which arises when sorting the sequence whose keys are:

   17   49   26   14   85   36   27   20   55   32   71

Note that at each node of the tree we have placed the keys of the (sorted) subsequence which will appear in *x* as a result of the call. To understand the procedure it is important to note that the two recursive calls inside *M* both interchange the parameters *x* and *y*. As the procedure is a postorder one, the actual sorting takes place from the leaves upwards.

Fig. 4.10. The tree of procedure calls for *MergeSort*.

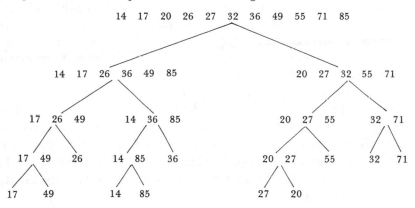

For completeness we give in Fig. 4.11 a fairly standard sequence for merging. We assume the relevant declarations of the variables it uses. Again ignore the values in the comments.

Fig. 4.11. A sequence for merging.

```
pl := 1; p2 := mid + 1; p := 1;              { b=4 }
repeat
  if y[pl].key < y[p2].key then              { c=3 }
    begin
    x[p] := y[pl]; pl := pl + 1;             { c=5 }
    tail := pl > mid                         { c=2 }
    end
```

77

```
    else
      begin
      x[p] := y[p2]; p2 := p2 + 1;                    { c=5 }
      tail := p2 > u                                  { c=7 }
      end;
    p := p + 1                                        { c=2 }
  until tail;                                         { c=1 }
  if pl <= mid then
    repeat
      x[p] := y[pl]; p := p + 1; pl := pl + 1
    until pl > mid
  else
    repeat
      x[p] := y[p2]; p := p + 1; p2 := p2 + 1
    until p2 > u
```

4.8   The analysis of *MergeSort*

Let us now analyse the *MergeSort* procedure, assuming for
the sake of simplicity, that n is a power of 2. (Note, however, that
the procedures themselves all work for any n and that in our example
sequence n has been deliberately chosen to be not a power of 2 to
underline the characteristics of the procedure being discussed.)

First we look at the merge sequence to determine the cost of
merging two sequences each of size $k/2$ into one of size k. Until one
of the sequences becomes empty, the repeat-loop is traversed once
for each element of the merged sequence. Further, each arm of the
if-statement which is the loop body contains similar orders. Thus
if it were not for having to deal explicitly with the tail of one
sequence when the other becomes exhausted, the cost would be of
the form $b+ck$, where b represents the initialisation and c the cost
of a traverse of the loop. In fact the cost of processing the tail has
a similar form, and to a first approximation we can assume that the
cost is simply $b+ck$.

Now considering *MergeSort* itself we immediately see that the
recurrence relation is of the form:

$$T_k = b + ck + 2T_{k/2}, \quad k \neq 1$$
$$\quad = a, \qquad\qquad\qquad k=1$$

Instead of deriving a solution, we prove that its solution is:

$$T_n = cn \log (n) + (a+b)n - b$$

First the explicitly specified case:

$$T_1 = c \times 1 \times \log(1) + (a+b) \times 1 - b$$
$$\quad = 0 + (a + b) - b$$
$$\quad = a$$

Now the general case:
$$T_n = b + cn + 2T_{n/2}$$
$$= b + cn + 2[\tfrac{1}{2}cn \log(\tfrac{1}{2}n) + \tfrac{1}{2}(a+b)n - b]$$
$$= b + cn + cn \log(\tfrac{1}{2}n) + (a+b)n - 2b$$
$$= b + cn + cn \log(n) - cn \log(2) + (a+b)n - 2b$$
$$= cn \log(n) + (a+b)n - b$$

Clearly the first term dominates and the procedure is $O(n \log(n))$.

We can express T_n a little more concretely in terms of fundamental operations. In Fig. 4.9 and Fig. 4.11 we have included the contributions to a, b and c of all the relevant statements. This leads to:
$$T_n = 13n \log(n) + 28n - 27$$
which excludes the cost of the copying within *MergeSort* and the initial call of *M*.

4.9   Investigating variations of *MergeSort*

In §4.4 we made the point that the recurrence relations and their solutions enable us to determine the effects of proposed changes to a procedure. We reinforce the point in this section.

If we look at *MergeSort* we notice that it uses the merging sequence to merge together subsequences of one element. We might reason that this is a sledge-hammer to crack a nut approach, and that instead we should stop the recursion one step earlier, merging the single-element sequences explicitly. In the light of our experience with the Towers of Hanoi we might hope for an improvement of about a factor of two.

We further notice that as the full sequences are in both x and y, the merging can be done very efficiently. Fig. 4.12 gives a modified version of the internal procedure *M*.

Fig. 4.12. A version of *M* stopping one level earlier.

```
procedure M(var x,y:seqtype; l,u:sizetype);
  var mid:sizetype;
  begin
  if u <= l + 1 then                     { a'=2, b'=2 }
    begin
    if y[l].key > y[u].key then          { a'=3 }
      begin
      x[l] := y[u]; x[u] := y[l]         { a'=6 }
      end
    end
  else
    begin
    mid := (l+u) div 2;                  { b'=3 }
```

```
        M(y,x,1,mid);                    { b'=9 }
        M(y,x,mid+1,u);                  { b'=10 }
        Merge(x,y,1,mid,u)               { As in Fig. 4.11 }
        end
    end { of procedure "M" };
```

The recurrence relations are:
$$T_k = b' + c'k + 2T'_{k/2}, \quad k \neq 2$$
$$= a', \qquad\qquad\quad k=2$$
whose solution is:
$$T'_n = c'n \log(n) + (\tfrac{1}{2}a' + \tfrac{1}{2}b' - c')n - b'$$
The appropriate values for the components of a' and b' are written on Fig. 4.12 and c' is the same as c of Fig. 4.11. If we assume that two consecutive elements are equally likely to be in order or out of order, then $a' = 6\tfrac{1}{2}$. We also have $b' = 28$ and $c' = 13$ which leads to:
$$T'_n = 13n \log(n) + 4\tfrac{1}{4}n - 28$$
as compared with:
$$T_n = 13n \log(n) + 28n - 27$$
for the original version.

For $n = 1000$, where $\log n \approx 10$, the comparison is approximately $134n$ as against $158n$, a gain of 15%; and for $n = 10\,000$ where $\log n \approx 32$, the comparison is approximately $420n$ as against $444n$, a gain of 5%.

This gain is acceptable, of course, but not as large as might have been expected in the light of having reduced the number of procedure calls by half. This simply underlines the meaning of:
$$T_n = cn \log(n) + (a+b)n - b$$
which is that the really worthwhile gain comes from reducing c. Since c is associated exclusively with the merging sequence, indeed with the inner loop, that is where the effort should be concentrated.

4.10 QuickSort

The objection to *MergeSort* is that it requires as much store again as the original sequence. In many operations this effectively reduces the number of items that can be sorted.

We consider now another $O(n \log (n))$ sorting method, *QuickSort*, which does not have this limitation. It is based on the notion of *partitioning*. We partition $x_l \to x_u$ into two sequences, the first $x_l \to x_{u1}$ containing items whose keys are less than or equal to some value (called the *partitioning key value*), the second $x_{l1} \to x_u$ containing items whose keys are greater than or equal to the partitioning key value. If these parts are not contiguous $x_{l1} \rightarrow x_{u1}$ contains items whose keys are equal to the partitioning key. We then recursively sort these subsequences. In Fig. 4.13 we give a procedure in which the partitioning sequence is as yet unspecified.

Fig. 4.13. A procedure for *QuickSort*.

```
procedure Quicksort(var seq:seqtype; n:sizetype);

    procedure Q(l,u:sizetype);
      var ll,ul:sizetype;
      begin
      if u <= 1 then { do nothing }
      else
         begin
         Partition(seq,l,u,ll,ul);
         Q(l,ul);
         Q(ll,u)
         end
      end { of procedure "Q" };

    begin
    Q(1,n)
    end { of procedure "Quicksort" };
```

In Fig. 4.14 we give the tree of procedure calls for *QuickSort*, to each node of which we have attached the keys of the (unsorted) subsequence which is in $x_l \rightarrow x_u$ at the call. We have yet to specify the partitioning sequence so the details may not be immediately clear but we have underlined the partitioning keys to help. Note that because the procedure is a preorder one, the actual sorting takes place from the root. Compare this with *MergeSort* (Fig. 4.10).

The partitioning sequence is based on scanning the array simultaneously from both ends. The lower bound of the upper subsequence $l1$ is set to l; and the upper bound of the lower sequence $u1$ is set to u. Then $l1$ is moved up over any item whose key is less than the partitioning key until it reaches one whose key is not. (Clearly all items that $l1$ moves over are correctly in the first subsequence.) Then $u1$ is moved down over any item whose key is greater than the partitioning key until it reaches one whose key is not. (Just as, clearly, all items that $u1$ moves over are correctly in the second subsequence.) For the given sequence and the partitioning value 36, we have the situation:

```
17   49   26   14   85   36   27   20   55   32   71
 ↑    ↑                                  ↑    ↑
 l    l1                                 u1    u
```

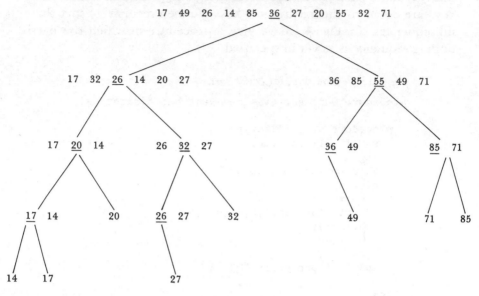

Fig. 4.14. A tree of procedure calls for *QuickSort*.

The elements at $l1$ and $u1$ are out of place. They are therefore interchanged and the pointers moved over them since they are now clearly in the correct subsequence. We have

17	32	26	14	85	36	27	20	55	49	71
↑		↑						↑		↑
l		$l1$						$u1$		u

This process is repeated until $u1$ and $l1$ cross.

The sequence in Fig. 4.15 is taken from Wirth (1976), who explains it in full detail. The reader is counselled not to make any seemingly obvious improvements until he has studied Wirth.

Fig. 4.15. The partitioning sequence.

```
ll := l; ul := u;
partkey := seq[(l+u) div 2].key;
repeat
  while seq[ll].key < partkey do ll := ll+1;
  while seq[ul].key > partkey do ul := ul-1;
  if ll <= ul then
    begin
    temp := seq[ll]; seq[ll] := seq[ul]; seq[ul] := temp;
    ll := ll+1;
    ul := ul-1
    end
until ll > ul
```

The analysis of *QuickSort* is essentially a statistical one, because its operation is so dependent on the data. As Fig. 4.14 illustrates the tree of procedure calls can be quite irregular varying from a perfectly balanced one to a completely unbalanced one (one in which each node except the leaves has a null branch).

The analysis of these two extremes, however, is quite straight-forward. From Fig. 4.15 we see that the partitioning involves a constant part, a part proportional to the size of the sequence $u-l+1$ and a part proportional to the number of interchanges required. It seems reasonable to assume that the number of interchanges is proportional to the size of the sequence.

For the perfectly balanced case, assuming k to be a power of 2 we have:

$$T_k = b + ck + 2T_{k/2}, \quad k \neq 1$$
$$= a \qquad\qquad\qquad k = 1$$

which is the same as that for *MergeSort*. We know its solution already:

$$T_n = cn \log(n) + (a+b)n - b$$

Perusal of the partitioning sequence shows that unless the number of interchanges is a large fraction of k, c will be less than 13, making the procedure faster than *MergeSort*.

For the degenerate case the relations are:

$$T_k = b + ck + T_{k-1}, \quad k \neq 1$$
$$= a, \qquad\qquad\qquad k = 1$$

which is the same as that for *SelectionSort*. Its solution is:

$$T_n = \tfrac{1}{2}cn^2 + (b+\tfrac{1}{2}c)n + (a-b-c)$$

Happily, on average *QuickSort* is $O(n \log(n))$ though we do not prove it here. The reader is referred to Knuth (1973) for the details.

4.11 Heaps and *HeapSort*

Perhaps this is the place to introduce another $O(n \log(n))$ sorting method, *heap sorting*, even though it is based directly on binary trees, and involves only linear recursion.

A *heap* is a balanced binary tree in which the key of an item at a node is greater than or equal to the keys of all the items on both its branches. Thus Fig. 4.16 is a heap containing the keys we have been using.

Heap sorting is a technique for sorting based on the use of a heap for organising the data. Clearly the item with the largest key is at the root and can be removed to become the largest element of the sorted

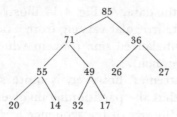

Fig. 4.16. A heap.

sequence. (Why this sequence is created in reverse will become clear in a few paragraphs.) If we can make the resulting pair of heaps (at the branches of the original root) into a heap again we can repeat the operation $n-1$ times to get the complete sorted sequence. To do this we detach the 'last' item (that is the rightmost item in the bottom level) and place it at the recently vacated root. Fig. 4.17(i) shows the situation. In general, as in Fig. 4.17, the result will not be

Fig. 4.17. Re-establishing the heap.

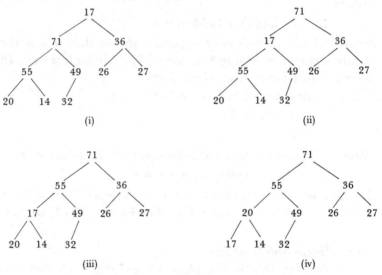

a heap, though it will be a balanced tree. We then compare the key of this item with the keys of the items on its two branches. If it is larger than both of them, then we have re-established the heap. If not we interchange it with the larger of the other two, as shown in Fig. 4.17(ii), and repeat the process, taking account of the fact that at some point a node might have only one branch or none at all. (See Fig. 4.17(iv).)

Now that we have re-established the heap, the item with the second largest key is at the root, and can be removed . . . .

Thus the sorting process can be expressed as:

for $i := n$ **downto 2 do**
begin
remove the item at the root;
re-establish the heap of size i
end

But of course we have to have the heap to start with. As a heap consists of two other heaps together with an item at the root whose key is larger than the keys of either heap, we must establish the heap from the bottom. Let us suppose that the items are initially put onto a balanced tree as shown in Fig. 4.18(i). Now the $n/2$ leaves are all heaps of one element each. The subtree whose root contains the item with a key of 85 is also a heap. That with a root

Fig. 4.18. Establishing the heap.

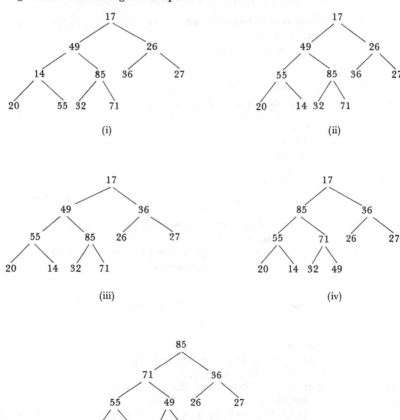

containing the item whose key is 14, is not, and so has to be reorganised as described earlier. The result is shown in Fig. 4.18(ii). The process continues as illustrated in Fig. 4.18 until the whole tree has become a heap, the same one as given in Fig. 4.16.

We could now write the complete procedure; but the same objection would be raised as was noted with respect to *MergeSort*: the procedure uses extra store for the pointers! However, a heap is a *balanced tree* and thus can be stored in an array without any pointers. The root is stored as $seq[1]$; its sons are stored as $seq[2]$ and $seq[3]$; and in general the sons of the node stored at $seq[i]$ are stored at $seq[2*i]$ and $seq[2*i+1]$. A null pointer is indicated by the fact that $2*i$ (or $2*i+1$) lies outside the bounds of the active part of the array. A procedure for *HeapSort* is given in Fig. 4.19.

Fig. 4.19. A procedure for *HeapSort*.

```
procedure Heapsort(var seq:seqtype; n:sizetype);
  var i:sizetype;
      temp:itemtype;


  procedure EstablishHeap(l,u:sizetype);
    var son:sizetype;
        temp:itemtype;
    begin
    if 2*l <= u then
      begin
      son := 2*l;
      if 2*l < u then { there is a right son }
        if seq[son].key < seq[son+1].key then
          son := son+1;
      if seq[l].key < seq[son].key then
        begin
        temp := seq[l]; seq[l] := seq[son]; seq[son] := temp;
        EstablishHeap(son,u)
        end
      end
    end { of procedure "EstablishHeap" };


  begin
  for i := n div 2 downto 1 do
    EstablishHeap(i,n);
  for i := n downto 2 do
    begin
    temp := seq[l]; seq[l] := seq[i]; seq[i] := temp;
    EstablishHeap(l,i-1)
    end
  end { of procedure "Heapsort" };
```

4.12 Recurrence relations: another cautionary tale

We made the point in Chapter 1 that it is unfortunately easy to write a very poor recursive procedure. A classical case arises with recurrence relations – the very things we have been using to analyse our procedures. Ours have been easily solved so that we could calculate $T(372)$, for example, directly. But consider the Fibonacci numbers, whose definition is:

$$
\begin{aligned}
Fib\,(n) &= 0, & n &= 0 \\
&= 1, & n &= 1 \\
&= Fib\,(n{-}1) + Fib\,(n{-}2), & n &> 1
\end{aligned}
$$

Thus the first ten Fibonacci numbers are:

$$0 \quad 1 \quad 1 \quad 2 \quad 3 \quad 5 \quad 8 \quad 13 \quad 21 \quad 34$$

The obvious function of Fig. 4.20 is woefully inefficient.

Fig. 4.20. A woefully inefficient function for Fibonacci numbers.

```
function Fib(n:natural):natural;
  begin
  if n <= 1 then Fib := n
  else Fib := Fib(n-1) + Fib(n-2)
  end { of function "Fib" };
```

The reason for its poor performance is clearly illustrated by the tree of procedure calls for $Fib\,(4)$ given in Fig. 4.21.

Fig. 4.21. The tree of procedure calls in evaluating $Fib\,(4)$.

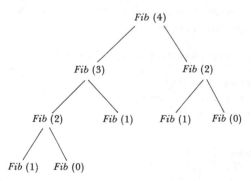

We see that we evaluate $Fib\,(2)$ twice and $Fib\,(1)$ three times! There is an obvious iterative solution, of $O(n)$, based on the storing at any time of the last two Fibonacci numbers calculated. This is given in Fig. 4.22.

87

Fig. 4.22. An iterative function for Fibonacci numbers.

```
function Fib(n:natural):natural;
  var penultimate,last,this,i:natural;
  begin
  if n <= 1 then Fib := n
  else
    begin
    last := 0; this := 1;
    for i := 2 to n do
      begin
      penultimate := last;
      last := this;
      this := penultimate + last
      end;
    Fib := this
    end
  end { of function "Fib" };
```

Clearly the iterative version is superior to the recursive one, and many authors stop here regarding this as one of those cases where a recursive version is inherently less efficient than a non-recursive version.

Of course this is not the case, since we are not comparing like with like. The non-recursive version uses information accumulated during the computation whereas the recursive procedure does not. Thus it is the difference in algorithm rather than the difference in control structure that accounts for the difference in complexity. We can easily construct a recursive version which uses the better algorithm and which as a consequence is $O(n)$. One is given in Fig. 4.23.

Fig. 4.23. An $O(n)$ recursive function for Fibonacci numbers.

```
function Fib(n:natural):natural;

  function F(i,last,this:natural):natural;
    begin
    if i = n then F := this
    else F := F(i+1,this,last+this)
    end { of function "F" };

  begin
  if n <= 1 then Fib := n
  else Fib := F(1,0,1)
  end { of function "Fib" };
```

We may think of the inner procedure's job as calculating $Fib(i+1)$ given that $Fib(i) = this$ and $Fib(i-1) = last$.

Note the importance of the parameters of F. They are used effectively to accumulate the values required for the calculation.

This technique has quite wide applicability as we shall illustrate by giving another $O(\log(n))$ procedure for *Power*.

Consider the evaluation of x^{13} by halving and squaring. The procedure of Fig. 1.19 involved squaring x^6 and multiplying by x. It found x^6 recursively, by squaring x^3 and so on. An alternative is to calculate x^{13} as $x^1 \times x^4 \times x^8$, where x^8, for example, is calculated by squaring x^4. Such a procedure is given in Fig. 4.24.

Fig. 4.24. Another $O(\log n)$ function *Power*.

```
function Power(x:real; n:integer):real;

  function P(k:natural; factor,sofar:real):real;
    begin
    if k = 0 then P := sofar
    else if odd(k) then P := P(k div 2,sqr(factor),sofar*factor)
    else P := P(k div 2,sqr(factor),sofar)
    end { of function "P" };

  begin
  if x = 0 then Power := 0
  else if n < 0 then Power := 1/P(-n,x,1)
  else Power := P(n,x,1)
  end { of function "Power" };
```

Note that both these procedures are preorder and can be easily converted to non-recursive procedures as we shall see in Chapter 8. Indeed the non-recursive version of *Fib* is precisely that given earlier in this section.

4.13   Generating binary code sequences

As a final example consider the generation of all 2^r possible patterns of r binary digits. For example for $r=3$ we might produce either of the sequences of Fig. 4.25.

Fig. 4.25 Two code sequences of three binary digits.

000	000
001	001
010	011
011	010
100	110
101	111
110	101
111	100

The first is the normal binary code, the second a reflected binary code. We consider the normal code. Note that it is in two halves, the first half containing codes starting with 0, the second containing codes starting with 1. Furthermore, taking the top half, if we rub out the 0 we are left with a two-bit code with the same property. Fig. 4.26 illustrates this by means of a tree.

Fig. 4.26. The generation of the three-bit normal binary code.

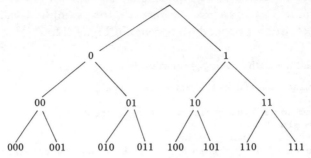

Suppose we wish to generate all 2^r codes in turn in an array, s say, and process them in a manner which we leave unspecified. A procedure to do this will, in general, make the choice 0 as the first element, store it in $s[1]$ and call itself recursively to produce the half of the codes that start with 0. Then it will make the choice 1 and call itself recursively to produce the other half. When it is choosing the rth element of course it will stop the recursion and process the code instead.

Fig. 4.27 gives a procedure in which we have abandoned our convention for naming an inner procedure and have used *Choose* instead. This reflects the way we think of the inner procedure as the means of organising the choice of the dth element of s.

The procedure assumes the definition:

   type *range* $= 1..nmax$;

where *nmax* is an appropriate constant.

Fig. 4.27. A procedure for generating the normal binary code.

```
procedure BinaryCodes(r:range);
  var s:array[range] of 0..1;

  procedure Choose(d:range);
    begin
    s[d] := 0;
    if d <> r then Choose(d+1) else Process(s);
    s[d] := 1;
    if d <> r then Choose(d+1) else Process(s)
    end { of procedure "Choose" };

  begin
  Choose(1)
  end { of procedure "BinaryCodes" };
```

This procedure is generally used with a recursive procedure for processing *s* as we shall see in the next chapter.

EXERCISES

4.1 Investigate the effects of each of the following changes to the *Hanoi* procedure of Fig. 4.4.
   (i) Replacing the writeln-statement in the general sequence by a recursive call $H(1, 1, 2, 3)$.
   (ii) Eliminating the fourth parameter $p3$, and using the fact that $p1+p2+p3=6$ to calculate it instead.
   (iii) Stopping the recursion when there are two rings to be moved.

4.2 The solution to the Towers of Hanoi problem given in the text assumes that the *pegs* are numbered, and the complete description is in those terms. Thus $1{\to}3$ is interpreted as move the (top) ring from peg 1 to (become the top ring of) peg 3. An alternative view is to assume that the *rings* are numbered from the smallest to the largest starting at 1. We can then describe moves by indicating the ring to be moved and its direction. For convenience we will describe the directions as clockwise (C), and anticlockwise (A), thinking of the towers as being in a triangular formation with the pegs numbered anticlockwise. Thus the following are two alternative descriptions of moving a tower for $n=3$.

$1{\to}3$	$1C$
$1{\to}2$	$2A$
$3{\to}2$	$1C$
$1{\to}3$	$3C$
$2{\to}1$	$1C$
$2{\to}3$	$2A$
$1{\to}3$	$1C$

Write a procedure to produce the alternative description of the moves based on the observations:
   (i) If we can move a tower of k rings in either direction we can certainly move a tower of $k+1$ rings by:
      (*a*) moving the top k rings in the opposite direction;
      (*b*) moving ring $k+1$ in the correct direction;
      (*c*) moving the top k rings again in the opposite direction.
   (ii) We can trivially move one ring.

4.3 Solve the recurrence relations

(i) $T_k = b + T_{k-1}, \quad k\neq0$

$ = a, \qquad\qquad k=0$

(ii) $T_k = b + 2T_{k-1}, \quad k\neq0$

$ = a, \qquad\qquad\ \ k=0$

(iii) $T_k = b + kT_{k-1}, \quad k\neq0$

$ = a, \qquad\qquad\ \ k=0$

(iv) $T_k = b + nT_{k-1}, \quad k\neq0$

$ = a, \qquad\qquad\ \ k=0$

4.4 Prove that the solution of:

$T_k = b + ck + 2T_{k/2}, \quad k\neq2$

$ = a, \qquad\qquad\quad\ k=2$

is:

$T_n = cn \log(n) + (\tfrac{1}{2}a+\tfrac{1}{2}b-c)n - b$

4.5 Modify the *MergeSort* procedure, Fig. 4.9, so that it explicitly sorts sequences of length $\leqslant8$ by some simple sorting techniques (such as linear selection (Fig. 4.8) or insertion sort). Assuming the size n to be a power of 2 analyse the procedure and compare it with the original.

4.6 There is a related *MergeSort* algorithm which is generally programmed iteratively. The sequence is regarded as n subsequences of length 1, and pairs of the subsequences are merged in turn to provide $\lfloor n/2 \rfloor$ subsequences of length 2 (possibly with a subsequence of length 1 left over). Pairs of these subsequences are merged to produce subsequences of length 4 and so on. Fig. 4.28 gives a tree representation of

Fig. 4.28. The action of the iterative *MergeSort*.

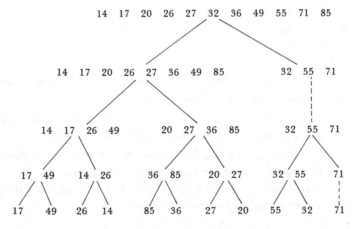

the process. Write an iterative procedure and compare it with *MergeSort* of Fig. 4.9. Also write a recursive version of this algorithm. Note that for this recursive procedure Fig. 4.28 may be interpreted as the tree of procedure calls in the same way as Fig. 4.10.

4.7 Write a procedure for generating Fibonacci numbers of $O(\log(n))$ by creating pairs of consecutive Fibonacci numbers based on the observations:

$$F_{2i} = (F_i + 2F_{i-1}) * F_i$$
$$F_{2i-1} = F_i^2 + F_{i-1}^2$$
$$F_{2i-2} = (2F_i - F_{i-1}) * F_{i-1}$$

4.8 Write a procedure for generating the reflected binary code of §4.13. Note that we choose the values for a given position to be the value we chose last time, followed by the other choice. This implies that the main procedure must first set all elements of s to 0.

5

Double recursion, mutual recursion, recursive calls

So far we have considered only the simple situation of procedures in which one form of recursion appeared. In this chapter we are going to consider problems in which recursion is required for two purposes, and for which it is tedious and difficult to produce solutions without the use of this *double recursion*.

We are also going to consider procedures in which the recursive call of a procedure A does not appear directly within A, as has been the case so far, but within some other procedure X which has been called, perhaps directly, perhaps indirectly, from A. Thus we may have a chain of calls $A \rightarrow B \rightarrow C \ldots X \rightarrow A$. This situation is called *indirect recursion* or *mutual recursion* in contrast with the *direct recursion* of the simple case.

Finally we are going to consider procedures which are, of themselves, non-recursive but which can give rise to recursion when called in a particular way.

5.1 An example of double recursion: determining tautology

Let us start with the double recursion and consider the problem of determining whether a logical expression such as:

$$p \land q \supset p \lor \neg p \land q$$

is tautologous: that is whether it is true for all possible combinations of its variables. We can see that there are two problems: firstly, we must be able to generate all possible combinations of a number of logical or Boolean variables; secondly, we must be able to evaluate a logical expression given the values of its variables. We have considered such problems before in Chapters 4 and 3 respectively and so we can proceed fairly directly.

First we generate the Boolean values. This is closely related to the procedure *BinaryCodes* of Fig. 4.27 with the type *Boolean* replacing the type $0..1$. The transformed version called *AllBooleans* is given in Fig. 5.1.

Fig. 5.1. Generating all combinations of r Boolean variables.

```
procedure AllBooleans(r:range);
  var s:array [range] of Boolean;

  procedure Choose(d:range);
    begin
    s[d] := false;
    if d <> r then Choose(d+1) else Process(s);
    s[d] := true;
    if d <> r then Choose(d+1) else Process(s)
    end { of procedure "Choose" };

  begin
  Choose(1)
  end { of procedure "AllBooleans" };
```

Now, we evaluate the expression. We assume that it is stored in a tree as shown symbolically in Fig. 5.2, where we have assumed the traditional precedences of the operators.

Fig. 5.2. The representation of $p \wedge q \supset p \vee \neg p \wedge q$.

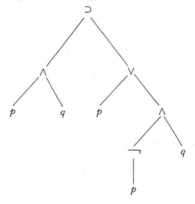

To be compatible with the generation of the Boolean values we assume that the variables p and q have been associated with entries in the array s and have been replaced by the integers 1 and 2 respectively. (This is just the process of lexical analysis.) Further, we assume a definition of this tree closely related to that of §3.8. In this case there is no need to cater for a Boolean constant, nor for the possibility of more than one unary operator. Note the use of the letter l (for logical) in the constant identifiers to avoid clashes with the Pascal reserved words *not, or, and*.

95

```
type treeptr =  ↑node;
     tagtype = (variable, lnot, binary);
     node =     record
                case tag : tagtype of
                variable : (index : range);
                lnot : (branch : treeptr);
                binary : (left : treeptr;
                            binop : (land, lor, impl);
                            right : treeptr)
          end
```

We could evaluate the logical expression along the lines of the arithmetic expression evaluation of Chapter 3, too. However, with logical expressions we can take advantage of the fact that often we know the value of an expression after evaluating only part of it. Thus in $E1 \wedge E2$, if $E1$ is false then so is the whole expression: therefore it is pointless to evaluate $E2$. For the three binary operators we have the following equivalences:

$E1 \wedge E2 \equiv$ if $E1$ then $E2$ else *false*
$E1 \vee E2 \equiv$ if $E1$ then *true* else $E2$
$E1 \supset E2 \equiv$ if $E1$ then $E2$ else *true*

The procedure of Fig. 5.3 follows.

Fig. 5.3. A procedure for evaluating a logical expression.

```
function ExprValue(t:treeptr):Boolean;
  var e:Boolean;
  begin
  case t↑.tag of
  variable:
    ExprValue := s[t↑.index];
  lnot:
    ExprValue := not ExprValue(t↑.branch);
  binary:
    begin
    e := ExprValue(t↑.left);
    case t↑.binop of
    land:if e then ExprValue := ExprValue(t↑.right)
         else ExprValue := false;
    lor: if e then ExprValue := true
         else ExprValue := ExprValue(t↑.right);
    impl:if e then ExprValue := ExprValue(t↑.right)
         else ExprValue := true
    end { of cases on "t↑.binop" }
    end { of case "binary" }
  end { of cases on "t↑.tag" }
  end { of procedure "ExprValue" };
```

We now have to put these two together to produce a Boolean procedure called, say, *Tautology*. It seems natural that we should generate all possible patterns of the variables, and as a pattern is generated call *ExprValue* to find the value of the expression for the current set of values of the variables. We will therefore convert the procedure *AllBooleans* into a Boolean function *Tautology* in which we shall nest the function *ExprValue*. The function *Tautology* will have the heading:

function *Tautology*(*t* : *treeptr*;*r* :*range*) :*Boolean*

where the parameter *t* points to the tree of the expression being tested.

An expression *t* is a tautology if and only if *t* is true for all possible combinations of values of its arguments. We could therefore modify *AllBooleans* by first of all initialising a local variable *v*, say, to *true*, by replacing *Process*(*s*) by the statement *v* := *v* and *ExprVal*(*t*), and by assigning *v* to *Tautology* immediately after the call *Choose*(1).

However, we can again capitalise on the properties of **and** so that *ExprVal*(*t*) is called only as long as all previous calls have produced the value *true*. To do this we could recast the for-loop as a while-loop. Instead we choose to jump right out of all the recursive activations of *Choose* if *ExprVal*(*t*) produces the value *false*. Fig. 5.4 gives the function.

Fig. 5.4. A function for determining whether a logical expression is a tautology.

```
function Tautology(t:treeptr; r:range):Boolean;
  label 1;
  var s:array [range] of Boolean;

  { As in Fig. 5.3 }

  procedure Choose(d:range);
    begin
    s[d] := false;
    if d <> r then Choose(d+1)
    else if not ExprValue(t) then goto 1;
    s[d] := true;
    if d <> r then Choose(d+1)
    else if not ExprValue(t) then goto 1
    end { of procedure "Choose" };

  begin
  Tautology := false;
  Choose(1);
  Tautology := true;
1:end { of function "Tautology" };
```

97

It should be noted that this is one of the more important uses of a goto-statement.

5.2   An example of mutual recursion: creating expression trees

We consider now mutual recursion – in which a number of procedures, here three, call each other in sequence with the last calling the first.

We have given a number of procedures for processing binary expression trees, either arithmetic or logical. We now see how such a tree might be created from a string of characters. For simplicity we will produce a tree whose items are all characters, the sort of tree we used in the early part of Chapter 3. The definition we use is:

> **type** *treeptr* = ↑*node*;
>   *node* = **record**
>   *left* : *treeptr*;
>   *item* : *char*;
>   *right* : *treeptr*
>   **end**

and we adopt the convention that a unary operator (here only —) has a null right branch. Furthermore we assume, for the moment, that there are no spaces within the characters of the expression and that *input*↑ initially holds the first character.

We will start in the middle and consider first how we might create the tree for a *term* given that we have a procedure which creates a tree for a *factor*.

We approach the problem by cases, starting with the simplest:

 (i) Suppose the term consists simply of a factor. The tree for the term is just that for the factor.

 (ii) Suppose the term consists of the product (or quotient) of only two factors. The tree for this term consists of a node whose item is * (or /) and whose left and right branches point to the trees for the two factors.

 (iii) Suppose the term consists of the product of three terms. (The terminology involved when we consider division is too convoluted to continue with. The implementation though is trivial.) The tree for this term consists of a node whose item is *, whose left branch points to the tree for the product of the first two factors, as described in (ii) above, and whose right branch points to the tree for the third factor.

 (iv) The general case obviously follows.

From this description we can easily create the procedure of Fig. 5.5 in which, as in Chapter 3, *NewTree(t,t,input↑,nil)* is a convenient shorthand for a sequence that creates a new node, pointed to by *t*, whose fields are (the old value of) *t*, *input↑*, and **nil**.

Fig. 5.5. A procedure for creating the tree for a term.

```
procedure Term(var t:treeptr);
  begin
  Factor(t);
  while input↑ in ['*','/'] do
    begin
    NewTree(t,t,input↑,nil);
    get(input) {  over the '*' or '/' };
    Factor(t↑.right)
    end
  end { of procedure "Term" };
```

The procedure for creating the tree for an expression, given this procedure, is similar but we have to consider the possibility of unary minus and create the appropriate node, one with '—' as item and with a null right branch.

We consider now the procedure for *Factor*. This creates the leaves. It also has to deal with the case of a bracketed expression which, of course, introduces the mutual recursion. Finally, because it creates the leaves it is the one that detects faulty expressions.

A procedure for the complete job is given in Fig. 5.6 in which we have chosen to nest *Factor* within *Term* within *Expression*.

Fig. 5.6. A procedure for creating an expression tree.

```
procedure Expression(var t:treeptr);

  procedure Term(var t:treeptr);

    procedure Factor(var t:treeptr);
      begin
      if input↑ in ['a'..'z','0'..'9'] then
        begin
        NewTree(t,nil,input↑,nil);
        get(input) { over the letter or digit }
        end
      else if input↑ = '(' then
        begin
        get(input) { over the opening parenthesis };
        Expression(t);
        if input↑ = ')' then
          get(input) { over the closing parenthesis }
        else error { closing parenthesis missing }
        end
```

```
          else error { letter, digit or opening parenthesis
                                    expected }
          end { of procedure "Factor" };

     begin { of procedure "Term" }
     Factor(t);
     while input↑ in ['*','/'] do
       begin
       NewTree(t,t,input↑,nil);
       get(input) {  over the '*' or '/' };
       Factor(t↑.right)
       end
     end { of procedure "Term" };

  begin { of procedure "Expression" }
  if input↑ = '-' then
     begin
     NewTree(t,nil,'-',nil);
     get(input) {  over unary minus };
     Term(t↑.left)
     end
  else
     Term(t);
  while input↑ in ['+','-'] do
     begin
     NewTree(t,t,input↑,nil);
     get(input) { over the '+' or '-' };
     Term(t↑.right)
     end
  end { of procedure "Expression" };
```

The procedure of Fig. 5.6 assumes that the expression being
input neither contains nor is preceded by spaces when *Expression*
is called. This restriction can be relaxed quite simply by replacing
input↑ and *get* by a variable, *ch*, and a procedure *Getch* which puts
the next non-space character into *ch* by reading over all intervening
spaces.

The procedure also assumes that the operands of the expression
are single characters. For symbolic manipulation, this is too restrictive. While we might accept single letters for the names of variables,
we would certainly wish to be able to use arbitrarily large constants
and, of course, to do arithmetic on them. To allow this we must
differentiate as we read between a variable and a constant and,
for a constant, read in the characters and evaluate it. Whether this is
done explicitly in *Factor*, or whether the procedure *Getch* is expanded
and renamed to include this function is a matter of taste. The precise
details of these changes depend on the form of structure chosen for
the tree – for example whether the leaves have **nil** branches or
none at all.

Further, there are many examples, such as the expression evaluation of Fig. 3.23 and the tautology determiner of Fig. 5.4, where we would like to be able to have multi-character identifiers as well and to associate these with the integers 1, 2, ... To do so, *Getch*, or as we shall now call it, *GetSym*, can be further expanded, reading in the characters of the identifier, adding them to a list (if they are not already there) and setting *sym* (a two-field record replacing *ch*) to indicate firstly that the symbol read is an identifier, and secondly what its associated integer is.

It is clear from this description that *GetSym* is essentially a lexical analyser. This explains the use of the word *symbol* and the letters *sym* in this description.

5.3 Another example: Sierpinski curves

On the cover of this book, and indeed of all books in this series, is a pattern based on the Sierpinski space-filling curves. There is an (infinite) series of such curves, and on the cover two are superimposed and stylised. In Fig. 5.7 we give the curves, separated, of order 1 to 4.

Fig. 5.7. Sierpinski curves of orders 1 to 4.

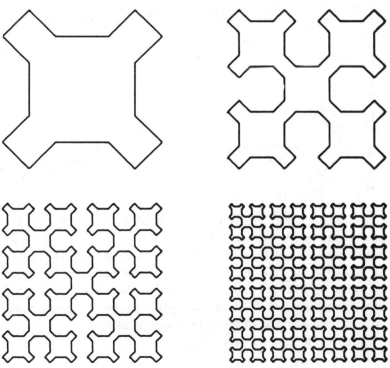

It is clear that a curve of order i can be created from one of order $i-1$. For example we could place four half-size versions of the simpler version in a square, join them together with two vertical and two horizontal lines and then rub out the sloping lines that are joined by these new lines.

However, it is difficult to get a graph plotter to rub out lines. Furthermore we wish to be able to draw a curve of order n by one continuous line, and so we must use a different approach. The following description and procedure is based on that of Wirth (1976).

The algorithm is simple once we realise that a curve consists of four components joined at the corners. In Fig. 5.8 we illustrate this with respect to curves of order 1. We will draw the curves in a clockwise direction starting in the bottom left-hand corner and will name the components N, E, S, W reflecting the direction in which they are drawn.

Note that all vertical and horizontal lines in a curve of a given order are of the same length, say $2h$, and the sloping lines are of length $\sqrt{(2)}h$.

Fig. 5.8. The components of Sierpinski curves.

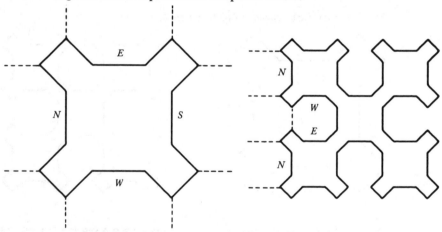

Now the components of a curve of order i are each made from the components of the curve of order $i-1$, joined by oblique and horizontal or vertical lines. Fig. 5.8 also shows, for example, that in drawing the N component of a curve of order i we draw curves of order $i-1$ in the sequence N, E, W, N joining them with lines in the directions NE, N, and NW respectively. A component curve of order 1 consists just of the three joining lines.

Suppose we use the notation:

  LineNE

to mean draw a line of length $\sqrt{(2)}h$ in a north-easterly direction,

> *LineN*

to mean draw a line of length $2h$ in a northerly direction, and define:

> type $order = 1..maxorder$

where *maxorder* is a constant related to the resolution of the plotter. Then an appropriate procedure for N is given in Fig. 5.9.

Fig. 5.9. A procedure for drawing a north component.

```
procedure N(i:order);
  begin
  if i = 1 then
    begin
    LineNE; LineN; LineNW
    end
  else
    begin
    N(i-1); LineNE;
    E(i-1); LineN;
    W(i-1); LineNW;
    N(i-1)
    end
  end { of procedure "N" };
```

Clearly the procedures for E, W and S are closely related and could be written down by inspection. The main procedure too follows from the description. The procedure of Fig. 5.10 then draws a Sierpinski curve of order i and size p. The size is measured in the units of the plotter used. Thus if the maximum range of the plotter is *maxsize* units then:

> type $size = 1..maxsize$

The procedures *StartPlot* and *StopPlot*, which we do not specify, perform the appropriate housekeeping; and $StartLine(x,y)$ initialises the pen at co-ordinates (x,y).

Fig. 5.10. A procedure for drawing a Sierpinski curve of order n.

```
procedure Sierpinski(i:order; p:size);
  var h:size;

  { The procedures N,E,S and W using Fig. 5.9
    as a model together with their forward
    declarations. }

  begin { of procedure "Sierpinski" }
  StartPlot;
  h := p div (power(2,i+2)-2);
  StartLine(0,round(h*sqrt(2)));
```

103

```
N(i); LineNE;
E(i); LineSE;
S(i); LineSW;
W(i); LineNW;
StopPlot
end { of procedure "Sierpinski" };
```

5.4 Variants of *Sierpinski* and its analysis

The reader will have noticed that the procedure N of Fig. 5.9 could be reduced in size by postulating a curve of order 0 whose components are null (and which therefore consists only of the four connecting lines, making a diamond shape).

The type *order* must be redefined:

type *order* $= 0..maxorder$

and when this is done we arrive at the procedure of Fig. 5.11.

Fig. 5.11. A more succinct procedure for drawing a north component.

```
procedure N(i:order);
  begin
  if i <> 0 then
    begin
    N(i-1); LineNE;
    E(i-1); LineN;
    W(i-1); LineNW;
    N(i-1)
    end
  end { of procedure "N" };
```

Let us now compare the two alternative versions of N by analysing them. We first of all recognise that N, E, S, W have the same form and the same cost. Then if:

$p = $ cost of a procedure call
$l = $ cost of a *Line* operation
$c = $ cost of a condition

We have for the original procedure:

$$T_i = 4p + 3l + c + 4T_{i-1}, \quad i > 1$$
$$= 3l + c, \quad i = 1$$

and for the succinct version:

$$T_i' = 4p + 3l + c + 4T_{i-1}, \quad i > 0$$
$$= c \quad i = 0$$

The solutions of these recurrence relations can be produced by substitution to give:

$$T_n = 4^n(p/3) + 4^n(c/3) + 4^n(l)$$
$$+ \{\text{small constants}\}$$

104

$$T_n' = 4^{n+1}(p/3) + 4^{n+1}(c/3) + 4^n(l)$$
$$+ \{\text{small constants}\}$$

(Of course, since Sierpinski calls N, E, S and W in turn, these figures have to be multiplied by 4 but we can safely ignore that fact in the comparisons.)

Thus the number of *Line* operations is the same (the same curve is being drawn) but the succinct version has four times the number of procedure calls and four times the number of tests. Thus if l is small, as it would be if the *Line* procedure simply wrote a record of three integers to a file, then the difference in cost of the two procedures might well be a factor of two. On the other hand, if the plotter were on line to the program, then l would dominate and the procedures would have approximately the same running time.

The reader might also have wondered whether the four procedures N, E, S, and W could be replaced by a single procedure. Indeed they can by giving the procedure (we shall now call it *NESW*) an extra parameter d say, of type *direction* defined:

type *direction* = (N,E,S,W)

The simplest solution would be for the procedure to consist of a case-statement, with d as the selector of one of the sequences which make up the bodies of the original procedures. However, these sequences can be merged into one if we parameterise the line drawing sequences. Suppose:

Oblique$(d1,d2)$

draws a line of length $\sqrt{(2)}h$ in one of the directions *NE*, *NW*, *SE* or *SW* as specified by $d1$ and $d2$; and

Ortho(d)

draws a line of length $2h$ in one of the directions N, E, S or W as specified by d. Then we can produce the procedure of Fig. 5.12, which, for simplicity is based on the succinct procedure of Fig. 5.11.

Fig. 5.12. Merging N, E, S and W into one procedure.
```
procedure NESW(d:direction; i:order);
  var dsucc,dpred:direction;
  begin
  if i <> 0 then
    begin
    if d = W then dsucc := N else dsucc := succ(d);
    if d = N then dpred := W else dpred := pred(d);
    NESW(d,i-1); Oblique(d,dsucc);
    NESW(dsucc,i-1); Ortho(d);
    NESW(dpred,i-1); Oblique(d,dpred);
    NESW(d,i-1)
    end
  end { of procedure "NESW" };
```

105

Clearly this procedure is less transparent than the four it replaces and is less efficient: there is an extra parameter to be transmitted, the original parameter has now to be calculated and the line drawing primitives are not ideally suited to most graph plotters. We would prefer to use the four separate procedures, especially as they are flexible enough to deal with less regular curves than those of Sierpinski, such as those of Hilbert. (See Wirth (1976) for these curves.)

5.5 Ackermann's function

We really cannot leave this subject without considering Ackermann's function. However, rather than produce it out of the blue, we show how it came to be created.

Let us restrict ourselves to natural numbers.

Consider first exponentiation. If we express multiplication by a function *Mult* instead of the operator *, and if we massage the explicitly defined case to use multiplication we then arrive at the procedure of Fig. 5.13.

Fig. 5.13. A function for the exponentiation of natural numbers.

```
function Power(x,n:natural):natural;
  begin
  if n = 0 then Power := Mult(1,1)
  else Power := Mult(x,Power(x,n-1))
  end { of function "Power" };
```

If we suppose that Pascal does not have multiplication built-in then we can define *Mult* in terms of addition as shown in Fig. 5.14.

Fig. 5.14. A function for multiplication of natural numbers.

```
function Mult(x,n:natural):natural;
  begin
  if n = 0 then Mult := Add(-1,1)
  else Mult := Add(x,Mult(x,n-1))
  end { of function "Mult" };
```

Similarly we could define *Add* in terms of the successor function, *succ*, which we might then explicitly program. (In Pascal, of course, it exists as a standard function.)

Now the procedures of Fig. 5.13 and Fig. 5.14 are very similar in the same way that N, E, S and W of the Sierpinski example are similar. Let us associate the integer 0 with *succ*, 1 with *add*, 2 with *mult* and 3 with *power*. Then we can express all the procedures as a single procedure using a further parameter m. This is done in Fig. 5.15 where we assume that $E1$ and $E2$ are expressions with the

106

appropriate values. (Since we are about to eliminate them it is wasteful to spell them out in detail.)

Fig. 5.15. A generalisation of *Mult* and *Power*.

```
function F(m,x,n:natural):natural;
  begin
  if m = 0 then F := E1
  else if n = 0 then F := F(m-1,E2,1)
  else F := F(m-1,x,F(m,x,n-1))
  end { of function "F" };
```

The Ackermann function given in Fig. 5.16 is an abstraction of this procedure in which $E1$ is set to $n+1$ and x is simply eliminated.

Fig. 5.16. Ackermann's function.

```
function Ack(m,n:natural):natural;
  begin
  if m = 0 then Ack := n+1
  else if n = 0 then Ack := Ack(m-1,1)
  else Ack := Ack(m-1,Ack(m,n-1))
  end { of function "Ack" };
```

Clearly this function uses recursion with a vengeance!

The real interest attached to Ackermann's function is theoretical: in the language of complexity theory it is a recursive function which is not primitive-recursive. However it also serves as a good test of the understanding of recursion: the reader might care to evaluate this function by hand for $m=2$, $n=3$. He may also like to calculate some values by running the procedure of Fig. 5.16. (Be careful! For $m=3$ this procedure effectively performs exponentiation by using only *succ*!)

5.6   Recursive calls

In all the examples so far used in this book, the recursion has been manifest. We can see simply by looking at the procedure that recursion is .involved, and, apart from specially constructed cases, a procedure or set of procedures is either recursive or not recursive.

However, recursion can also result through parametric procedures, in which case procedures which are not explicitly recursive are called recursively.

Let us suppose we have an integration procedure like that of §4.6 with a heading:

$$\textbf{function } Quad(\textbf{function } f(x:real):real; a,b:real):real$$

which has a value equal to $\int_a^b f(x)\,\mathrm{d}x$. We are not concerned with

107

how *Quad* operates, but for simplicity of the following description we assume that it is not adaptive. That is, it is not, of itself, recursive.

To use this procedure to evaluate:

$$y = \int_a^b e^x \cos x \, dx$$

we must first write a procedure which will evaluate the integrand given a value of x:

```
function ExpCos(x:real);
  begin
  ExpCos := exp(x)*cos(x)
  end
```

and then call *Quad* with that function and the two limits as arguments.

$$y := Quad(ExpCos,a,b)$$

Now suppose we wish to evaluate the double integral:

$$z = \int_{ax}^{bx} \int_{ay}^{by} F(x, y) \, dy \, dx$$

Here the integrand is itself an integral:

$$\int_{ay}^{by} F(x, y) \, dy$$

and we have to write a function, I say, that will evaluate this integral for given values of x. When we do so the double integral can be evaluated as before by:

$$z := Quad(I,ax,bx)$$

The function I is simply written as Fig. 5.17 shows.

Fig. 5.17. Evaluating a double integral.

```
function I(x:real):real;

  function J(y:real):real;
    begin
    J := F(x,y)
    end   { of function "J" };

  begin
  I := Quad(J,ay,by)
  end { of function "I" };
```

Note that *Quad* is now used recursively. The statement

$$z := Quad(I,ax,bx)$$

invokes *Quad* which, by calling the parameter f, calls I which again calls *Quad*.

108

Of course if *Quad* were adaptive as is *Integral* of Fig. 4.7 then it would be directly recursive too.

5.7 Substitution parameters

If we exclude for the moment parametric procedures and functions, Pascal has two classes of parameters, those called by value and those called as variables, whose characteristics are well under-stood. In this section we assume the existence of a further class, parameters called by substitution†, whose operation is as follows. Within a procedure, a formal parameter behaves as if the *text* of the actual parameter were substituted for it. Consider the procedure of Fig. 5.18 and assume the appropriate declarations of the quantities involved.

Fig. 5.18. A procedure to illustrate call by substitution.

```
procedure Ex(subst k,m:integer; subst x,y:real);
  begin
  for k := 1 to m do
    x := y
  end { of procedure "Ex" };
```

The call:

$$Ex(i, 1, p, 0)$$

causes the body to behave as:

```
begin
for i := 1 to 1 do
  p := 0
end
```

and so sets p to 0. (Of course, as a side-effect, i becomes undefined.)

The call:

$$Ex(i,n,a[i],a[i]+b[i])$$

causes the body to behave as:

```
begin
for i := 1 to n do
  a[i] := a[i] + b[i]
end
```

so that the vector b is added to the vector a. The implementation of substitution parameters does not involve actual textual substitution since, when the program is running, the text has been converted to binary. Instead an access of such a formal parameter is compiled into

† This is Algol's call-by-name parameter.

a sequence which determines the value (or the address in appropriate situations) of the actual parameter. In what follows it is easier to think in these terms rather than in terms of textual substitution, since textual substitution often produces syntactically invalid programs. Clearly an actual parameter may be an expression provided the corresponding formal parameter does not appear on the left-hand side of our assignment, either explicitly (as x in Fig. 5.17) or implicitly (as k).

Now consider the closely related function, called *GPS* by Knuth and Merner (1961), of Fig. 5.19.

Fig. 5.19. Knuth's *GPS* function.

```
function GPS(subst k,m:integer; subst x,y:real):integer;
  begin
  k := 1;
  while k <= m do
    begin
    x := y;
    k := k + 1
    end;
  GPS := 1
  end { of function "GPS" };
```

It is simply *Ex* recast so that it uses a while-statement and expressed as a function whose value is 1. Thus to set p to 0 we write:

$$dummy := GPS(i, 1, p, 0)$$

ignoring the assignment of 1 to *dummy*. Similarly

$$dummy := GPS(i,n,a[i],a[i]+b[i])$$

causes b to be added to a.

Now the fact that *GPS* is a function with the value 1 means that:

$$dummy := GPS(k,0*GPS(i,n,a[i],a[i]+b[i]),x,y)$$

where x and y are real variables also causes b to be added to a. Consider the outer call of *GPS*. Clearly its loop is not obeyed because its upper limit is 0. However, in determining this value, the inner call has to be evaluated, and this as we saw in the previous paragraph, causes b to be added to a.

From this observation we can see that:

$$dummy := GPS(i, (n-1)*GPS(j,n,a[i,j],a[i,j]+b[i,j]),x,y)$$

adds the *matrix* b to the *matrix* a. The outer call causes $n-1$ assignments of x to y with i being set to 1, 2... n. However in this loop the final value $(n-1)*GPS(j,n,a[i,j],a[i,j]+b[i,j])$ is evaluated n times. On each occasion the ith row of b is added to a.

Clearly, while the function *GPS* is not recursive, it is invoked recursively simply by its call.

It is interesting to note that this function is very powerful. Knuth and Merner state that any computable function can be expressed as a single call of *GPS*. Hence its name: an acronym for *General Problem Solver*.

EXERCISES

5.1 Modify the function *Tautology* of Fig. 5.4 so that it determines whether a logical formula is a tautology, a contradiction (i.e. it is false for all combinations of its arguments) or neither of these two.

5.2 Expand your tautology/contradiction determiner (Ex. 5.1) so that it reads in the expressions it tests.

5.3 Expand your differentiation program (Ex. 3.7) to read in the expressions if differentiates.

Fig. 5.20. W-curves of order 1 to 4.

5.4 Write a general package for reading in arithmetic expressions and simplifying them.

5.5 Write a program for a simple calculating language with two forms of statement, one for assigning a value to a variable and one for printing out an expression as illustrated below:
LET $X = 7$
LET $Y = 3$
PRINT $(X+Y)*(X-Y)/8$
This should result in 5 being printed.

5.6 Fig. 5.20 gives curves, due to Wirth (1976) who calls them W-curves, of order 1 and 4. Write a procedure to draw a curve of order n.

5.7 Consider the snowflake curves of Fig. 5.21. As the order increases, so does the perimeter (by a factor of $\frac{4}{3}$ each time) but the area slowly approaches a limiting value. Write a procedure to draw a curve of order n.

Fig. 5.21. The snowflake curves of order 1 to 4.

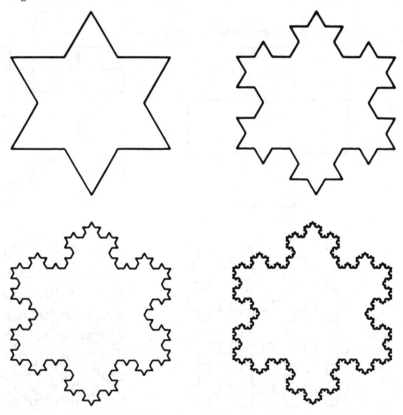

5.8 Analyse the *NESW* procedure of Fig. 5.12 to determine the
   extra cost involved in the use of that procedure rather than
   the *N*, *E*, *S* and *W* procedures of Fig. 5.11. Do the same
   for the version of Fig. 5.22 which is essentially that of
   Goldschlager (1981).

Fig. 5.22. An alternative *NESW* procedure.

```
procedure NESW(d1,d2,d3,d4:direction; i:order);
   begin
   if i <> 0 then
      begin
      NESW(d1,d2,d3,d4,i-1); Oblique(d1,d2);
      NESW(d2,d3,d4,d1,i-1); Ortho(d1);
      NESW(d4,d1,d2,d3,i-1); Oblique(d1,d4);
      NESW(d1,d2,d3,d4,i-1)
      end
   end { of procedure "NESW" };
```

5.9 Consider a generalisation of the Towers of Hanoi problem
   discussed in §4.1, in which a fourth peg is added (Rohl
   & Gedeon (1983)). Fig. 5.23 gives the inner procedure *H4*
   for generating a solution based on the use of the traditional
   procedure, here renamed *H3* to underline its applicability
   to the three-peg case. The function $f(n)$, which we leave
   undefined, determines the number of rings to be moved
   using only three pegs.

Fig. 5.23. The inner procedure of a four-tower *Hanoi* procedure.

```
procedure H4(n:ndiscs; p1,p2,p3,p4:pegtype);
   begin
   if n <> 0 then
      begin
      H4(n-f(n),p1,p4,p3,p2);
      H3(f(n),p1,p2,p3);
      H4(n-f(n),p4,p2,p3,p1)
      end
   end { of procedure "H4" };
```

Write a generalised procedure with the heading:

procedure $H(m:npegs, n:ndiscs; p:pegtype)$

to generate the solution for m pegs assuming the existence
of a function $f(m,n)$, whose value is the number of the
n rings to be moved using $m-1$ pegs. Note that *pegtype* is
now an array.

5.10 Use *Quad* to evaluate $\int_{ax}^{bx} \int_{ay}^{by} \int_{az}^{bz} f(x,y,z) \, \mathrm{d}z \, \mathrm{d}y \, \mathrm{d}x$.

5.11 Use *GPS* to:
    (i) perform the scalar product of two vectors;
   (ii) multiply two matrices;
 (iii) find the nth prime number.

6
Recursion with *n*-ary trees and graphs

In Chapter 2 we considered a very simple data structure, the linked-linear list; and in Chapter 3 we moved on to binary trees. In this chapter we look at two much more general structures.

Firstly we shall consider trees in which nodes may have more than two branches, and in which the number of branches may vary from node to node. For want of a better name we shall call them *n-ary* trees.

Secondly we shall consider even more general structures which arise when more than one branch leads into a node. These structures are called *directed graphs*. Clearly they are more general than *n*-ary trees, which, therefore, may be regarded as a special case.

6.1 B-trees

We consider first the *n*-ary tree, and, in this section, its use in searching applications. Such trees are usually called B-trees, a convention we shall follow.

When we discussed binary trees in Chapter 2 we noted that searching, insertion and deletion were all $O(\log n)$, provided that the tree remained balanced. Although we did not discuss the topic of balance in much detail there, we referred the reader to a number of relevant techniques. B-trees arise in this connection too, though here we shall approach them from a different point of view.

Let us imagine first of all that we have a sequence of variable-length items in the store with an item with an infinite key placed at the end.

Let us now provide an *index block*, that is a block containing, for each data item, its key and a reference to the item itself. Then the searching process can be decomposed into two parts: first search the index block to determine from the keys the appropriate data item, second access that item. Note that the items need not be contiguous in the store. Indeed they may be on the heap, a situation we will assume in what follows, or even on disk.

Finally let us suppose that the number of entries in the index block is kept between $n/2$ and n for some given value of n. In practice n might be a few hundred: in our diagrams it will be 4. Then, for a large enough number of items, we need a number of index blocks and an *index* of *index blocks* and so on. These higher level index blocks hold the *maximum* key of each of the index blocks they refer to. This structure of index blocks is called a B-tree and n is called its *order*.

Fig. 6.1 gives an example of a B-tree of order 4 containing the keys:

$$5 \quad 8 \quad 13 \quad 15 \quad 16 \quad 18 \quad 19 \quad 22 \quad 30 \quad 40 \quad 46 \quad 48 \quad 60 \quad 61 \quad 67$$

Note that the last key on any level is an 'infinite' one. We use this to aid the searching of blocks.

An appropriate definition of this structure is:

```
const n = {the order of the tree};
      nover2 = {n div 2};
type  tagtype = (index, data);
      sizetype = 1..n;
      itemtype = record
                   key : keytype;
                   info : infotype
                 end;
      Bptr = record
               maxkey : keytype;
               case tag : tagtype of
               index : (indexptr : ↑indextype);
               data : (itemptr : ↑itemtype)
             end;
      indextype = record
                    nbranches : sizetype;
                    branches : array [sizetype] of Bptr
                  end
```

Note that, when a branch refers to a data item, *maxkey* holds the value of the (only) key of that item.

It is clear that a B-tree is balanced by its very definition, and when we discuss insertion we will see that it expands at the root. That is, the initial blocks are on the same level, but as they increase in number it sometimes becomes necessary to add a new level of index block. Thus for N items its height ranges between $\log_n N$, when there

116

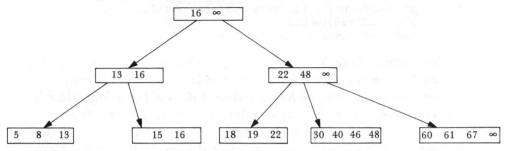

Fig. 6.1. A B-tree of order 4.

are precisely n entries to each index block, and $\log_{n/2} N$, when each block is only half full. At the early stages of creating a tree, when the number of items is less than $n/2$, then clearly the constraint on the number of items in a block cannot hold. However, if the tree has at least $n/2$ items, then the insertion procedure will ensure that it does hold. The constraint on the number of entries in an index block always holds for leaf and internal blocks but it may or may not hold for the root block.

6.2 The basic operations on B-trees

From the description given above it is fairly clear how a function for searching could be written. Let us assume the existence of a function, *IndexSub*, which searches an index block to find which lower level block must be searched next. More precisely its value is the smallest subscript of *branches* whose *maxkey* field is greater than or equal to the key being sought, k. Clearly this function can be produced by minor modifications to the *InArray* functions of Chapter 1.

Given this function, we can produce the function *OnBTree* as shown in Fig. 6.2.

Fig. 6.2. Searching a B-tree.

```
function OnBTree(B:Bptr; k:keytype):Boolean;

function O(B:Bptr):Boolean;
  var s:sizetype;
  begin
  with B.indexptr↑ do
    begin
    s := IndexSub(branches,nbranches,k);
    if branches[s].tag = data then
      O := k = branches[s].maxkey
    else
      O := O(branches[s])
    end
  end { of function "O" };
```

117

```
begin
if B.indexptr = nil then OnBTree := false
else OnBTree := O(B)
end { of function "OnBTree" };
```

The function *IndexSub* can use either a linear search (appropriate for small orders) or binary search (appropriate for larger orders).

Note, however, that *OnBTree* exhibits double recursion: there is the recursion involved in descending the tree, and the recursion involved in finding the appropriate branch to descend. This latter is linear and postorder, and can be easily made iterative. This is one of those cases referred to in §2.8 where we would prefer to use the iterative version. Further we would use the sequence directly rather than make it a function.

We move on now to insertion. As a new item is added we have to maintain the index blocks, perhaps creating a new level. We consider two cases in turn which we illustrate by inserting different keys into the tree of Fig. 6.1:

(i) A key of 20. We find and search the appropriate leaf block (here the third from the left) and insert it into the correct place, moving all larger keys (here only 22) to the right. The other index blocks need no modification. The result is shown in Fig. 6.3.

Fig. 6.3. The result of adding a key of 20 to the tree of Fig. 6.1.

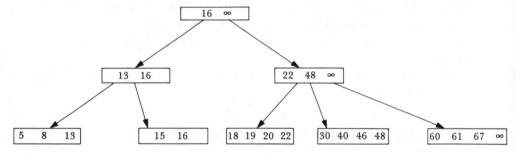

(ii) A key of 45. It must go into the fourth block from the left – but this is full. The solution is to 'split the node'. That is, a new block is created and placed in position just after the full one. Then the items in the full block are distributed equally across the two, the item added at the appropriate place in the appropriate block, and a new entry made in the index block above. Fig. 6.4 shows the result.

Note that two entries have changed in the middle-level index block on the right. A new key, 40, has been added with the appropriate

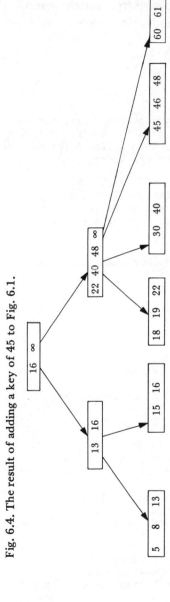

Fig. 6.4. The result of adding a key of 45 to Fig. 6.1.

reference to the leaf block; and the key 48 has been moved to the right and acquired a reference to the new leaf block.

It is clear that this splitting can propagate up the tree, as the index block in turn may be full just before one of its data block splits. If this reaches the root, then the splitting process involves the creation of a new root and the tree grows by a level.

Fig. 6.5, the *InsertOnBTree* procedure, which inserts a branch pointing to an item held on the heap, is written in a two-level form.

Fig. 6.5. Inserting a key onto a B-tree.

```
procedure InsertOnBTree(var B:Bptr; br:Bptr);
   var newbr,oldbr:Bptr;
      split:Boolean;

   procedure I(var B:Bptr; var split:Boolean; var newbr:Bptr);
      { This adds the branch on to the subtree B.  If as a result
      the root block is split, then split is set to true and
      newbr set to point to the new block. }
      var s:sizetype;

      procedure InsertInBlock(br:Bptr);
         { This actually inserts a branch br into the current block B,
         setting split and newbr appropriately. }
         var j:sizetype;
         begin
         { See if the block has to be split }
         split := B.indexptr↑.nbranches = n;
         if split then { create block }
            begin
            { Create new block from first half of old block. }
            newbr := B;
            with newbr,indexptr↑ do
               begin
               nbranches := nover2;
               maxkey := branches[nbranches].maxkey
               end;
            { Adjust the old block accordingly. }
            new(B.indexptr);
            with B,indexptr↑ do
               begin
               nbranches := nover2;
               for j := 1 to nbranches do
                  branches[j] := newbr.indexptr↑.branches[j+nover2]
               end
            end { of creating the block };
         { Now insert br into the right block }
         if not split or (s>nover2) then { in old block }
            with B.indexptr↑ do
               begin
               if split then s := s−nover2;
               for j := nbranches downto s do
                  branches[j+1] := branches[j];
               branches[s] := br;
               nbranches := nbranches+1
               end { of inserting in old block }
```

```
            else { in new block }
              with newbr.indexptr↑ do
                begin
                for j := nbranches downto s do
                  branches[j+1] := branches[j];
                branches[s] := br;
                nbranches := nbranches+1
                end { of inserting in new block }
            end { of procedure "InsertInBlock" };

      begin { of procedure "I" }
      with B.indexptr↑ do
        begin
        s := IndexSub(branches,nbranches,br.maxkey);
        if branches[s].tag = data then
          if br.maxkey = branches[s].maxkey then { already there }
            split := false
          else InsertInBlock(br)
        else { if branches[s].tag = index then }
          begin
          I(branches[s],split,newbr);
          if split then
            InsertInBlock(newbr)
          end
        end
      end { of procedure "I" };

begin { of procedure "InsertOnBTree" }
if B.indexptr = nil then { create initial tree }
  begin
  B.tag := index;
  new(B.indexptr);
  B.indexptr↑.nbranches := 1;
  B.indexptr↑.branches[1] := br;
  B.maxkey := br.maxkey
  end
else
  begin
  I(B,split,newbr);
  if split then { create new level }
    begin
    oldbr := B;
    new(B.indexptr);
    B.indexptr↑.nbranches := 2;
    B.indexptr↑.branches[1] := newbr;
    B.indexptr↑.branches[2] := oldbr
    end
  end
end { of procedure "InsertOnBTree" };
```

The deletion procedure for B-trees obviously follows similar
lines. However, this time the index blocks merge rather than split
as items are deleted. We leave it to the reader to create his own
version.

6.3 A discussion of B-trees

Our approach to B-trees through the notion of multi-level indexes is not the only one. An alternative is to view them as the result of flattening $\log_2 n$ levels of a binary tree into blocks. With this view it is natural to have *items* in the internal blocks, whereas with our representation we had only keys there. This is the approach usually adopted in texts on data structures. The structure of the processing procedures is simplified since they do not need to discriminate on the type of the block. We refer the reader to Wirth (1976) for the details.

B-trees find application in searching large sequences which by their very size have to be stored on external devices. For a tree of height h only $2h+1$ blocks ever have to be in store. Usually, of course, there will be h, but because of the merging and splitting processes, we sometimes have to create new blocks. At worst we have to create one for each of those searched plus one for a new root. If we assume that fetching blocks from external devices is slow, then the virtue of a tree of fixed height is manifest. Further the time taken searching through the blocks is probably insignificant.

B-trees are used for internal searching too, and simple forms of them such as 2–3 trees have already been referred to.

Of course, the searching, inserting and deleting procedures all exhibit only linear recursion provided, of course, that the searching through the blocks is done iteratively. However, consider the procedure for writing out the keys on a B-tree in order given in Fig. 6.6, which uses *WriteKey*, to write out the individual keys.

Fig. 6.6. Writing out a B-tree.

```
procedure WriteBTree(B:Bptr);
  var s:sizetype;
  begin
  if B.indexptr <> nil then
    with B.indexptr↑ do
      for s := 1 to nbranches do
        if branches[s].tag = data then
          WriteKey(branches[s].maxkey)
        else
          WriteBTree(branches[s])
  end { of procedure "WriteBTree" };
```

This exhibits *n-ary recursion*. That is, except at the bottom-level, the procedure calls itself a number of times, one for each branch. This number may well be large, and is certainly variable, and so the calls are performed in a loop. There is only one textual call, but it is obeyed repetitively.

122

6.4 *N*-ary expression trees

Let us now return to expressions. So far we have used binary expression trees, the internal nodes of which in general have two branches representing the binary nature of the operators involved such as + and −. (They also included nodes for unary operators which, of course, have only one branch.) An example is given on the left of Fig. 6.7 for the expression $h*(f0+4*f1+f2)*onethird$.

Fig. 6.7. Trees holding $h * (f0 + 4 * f1 + f2) * onethird$.

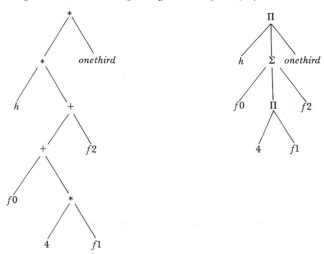

On the right is an *n*-ary tree for the same expression. The operators are sum, Σ, and product, Π, which in general have an arbitrary number of arguments, so that the tree has an arbitrary number of branches.

What is the advantage of the *n*-ary tree over the binary tree for expressions? It is simply that the *n*-ary tree *explicitly* reflects the *associative* nature of addition and multiplication. It is clear that the expression is a product of three quantities, two of which are h and *onethird*, the third being a sum of three quantities.

The same information is available in the binary tree, of course, but there it is *implicit*.

That this is an advantage can be simply demonstrated. Suppose we had produced, perhaps as the result of some manipulation, the binary tree of Fig. 6.8(i). It is not immediately clear that the 2 and the 1 could be combined as in Fig. 6.8(ii), this latter tree being of quite a different structure. Given the equivalent *n*-ary tree, Fig. 6.8(iii) to start with, the transformation to the tree of Fig. 6.8(iv) can hardly be missed. This is only the simplest example of the

123

Fig. 6.8. The advantage of *n*-ary trees.

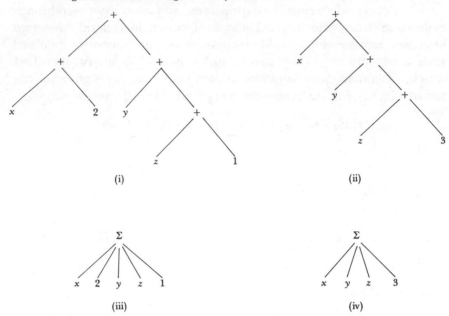

(i)   (ii)

(iii)   (iv)

advantages of *n*-ary trees: others include the ease with which compilers using them can produce more optimum code.

   To return, not all operators are associative so we cannot create
equivalent *n*-ary operators: it makes no sense to talk of the *difference
of three quantities*, for example. We must therefore allow *n*-ary trees
to include binary (and unary) nodes as appropriate. We will, however,
avoid the use of the subtraction operator by regarding subtraction
as the addition of the negative of the second operand. This allows it
to become an operand of Σ-node. Similarly we consider division
as multiplication by the reciprocal of the second operand. In Fig.
6.9 we give *n*-ary trees for $h*(f0+4*f1+f2)/3$ and $b\uparrow2-4*a*c$,
in which $-$ represents the unary negative operator and $\div$ the unary
reciprocal operator.

Fig. 6.9. *N*-ary trees for $h * (f0 + 4 * f1 + f2)/3$ and $b \uparrow 2 - 4 * a * c$.

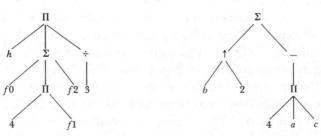

6.5 The storage of *n*-ary expression trees

The characteristic of the *n*-ary tree is that the number of branches of an *n*-ary node is variable, and this dominates the problem of how to store such trees. Let us suppose, firstly, that we can place some sensible upper limit on this number. This might be reasonable in a compiler, for example, since any expression being compiled is bound to be relatively short. Then the branches of such a node can be stored in an array. An appropriate definition, based on that for binary trees in §3.8, might be:

```
type range = 1. .max;
     tagtype = (constant,variable,unary,binary,nary);
     naryptr = ↑node;
     node = record
               case tag : tagtype of
               constant: (value : real);
               variable : (index : range);
               unary : (unop : (neg,recip);
                        branch : naryptr);
               binary : (left : naryptr;
                        binop : (expon);
                        right : naryptr);
               nary : (naryop : (sum,prod);
                        nbranches : sizetype;
                        branches : array [sizetype] of naryptr)
            end
```

where *sizetype* defines the range of the number of branches an *n*-ary node may have. Fig. 6.10 gives a pictorial representation of

Fig. 6.10. Storage of *n*-ary trees using arrays.

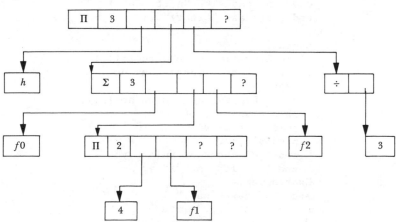

the storage of $h*(f0+4*f1+f2)/3$ using this definition. Note that the tag fields have been omitted, and that symbols have been used for all operators and operands for clarity. *Sizetype* is assumed to be 1..4.

Inasmuch as n-ary trees are an obvious extension of binary trees (or almost so) the processing of these trees in many ways is an obvious extension of the processing of binary trees. For example in Fig. 6.11 we give a function for evaluating an expression held in such a tree.

Fig. 6.11. Evaluating an expression held in an n-ary tree.

```
function ExprValue(n:naryptr):real;
  var vl,v2:real;
      i:sizetype;
  begin
  case n↑.tag of
  constant:
    ExprValue := n↑.value;
  variable:
    ExprValue := data[n↑.index];
  unary:
    begin
    vl := ExprValue(n↑.branch);
    case n↑.unop of
    neg:ExprValue := -vl;
    recip:ExprValue := 1/vl
    end { of cases on "n↑.unop" }
    end { of case "unary" };
  binary:
    begin
    vl := ExprValue(n↑.left);
    v2 := ExprValue(n↑.right);
    case n↑.binop of
    expon: ExprValue := Power(vl,v2)
    end { of cases on "n↑.binop" }
    end { of case "binary" };
  nary:
    begin
    vl := ExprValue(n↑.branches[1]);
    for i := 2 to n↑.nbranches do
      begin
      v2 := ExprValue(n↑.branches[i]);
      case n↑.naryop of
      sum:vl := vl+v2;
      prod:vl := vl*v2
      end { of cases on "n↑.naryop" }
      end { of loop on "i" };
    ExprValue := vl
    end { of case "nary" }
  end { of cases on "n↑.tag" }
  end { of function "ExprValue" };
```

Note that the sequence for processing a binary node is closely related to that for processing an *n*-ary node. We could in fact eliminate the notion of a binary node altogether, expanding the *n*-ary node to include it. While this would have simplified the *ExprValue* function, we chose not to do so, since the distinction is sometimes important: the operators at *n*-ary nodes are commutative, while those at binary nodes may not be. However in §6.6 we make the contrary decision so that the reader may decide for himself.

In many situations the use of an array would be unacceptable. In algebraic manipulation systems, the size of *n*-ary nodes varies quite markedly during the running of a program. The range specified by *sizetype* would have to be quite large and at any one time, most of the nodes would have many fewer branches. Thus an alternative would be to store the branches of an *n*-ary node in a list. An appropriate definition then might be:

```
type range = 1..max;
     tagtype = (constant,variable,unary,binary,nary);
     naryptr = ↑node;
     node = record
                 case tag : tagtype of
                 constant : (value : real);
                 variable : (index : range);
                 unary : (unop : (neg,recip);
                          branch : naryptr);
                 binary : (left : naryptr;
                           binop : expon;
                           right : naryptr);
                 nary : (naryop : (sum,prod);
                         branches : listptr)
            end
```

where:

```
listptr = ↑listnode;
listnode = record
               item : naryptr;
               next : listptr
           end
```

In Fig. 6.12 we give a pictorial representation of the storage of $h*(f0+4*f1+f2)/3$ using the same conventions as those of Fig. 6.10.

The *ExprValue* procedure of Fig. 6.11 is easily modified to operate with this structure: the for-statement which accesses the branches in turn from the elements of the array is replaced by

Fig. 6.12. Storage of n-ary trees using lists.

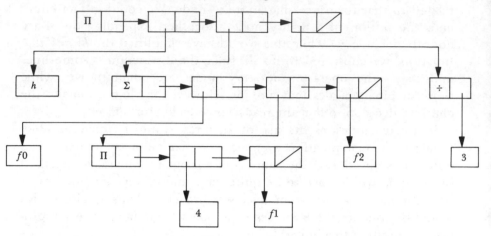

a while-statement which accesses them by sequencing through the list.

Reference to the diagram of Fig. 6.12 shows that the storage is dominated by space for pointers. The situation is worse than suggested by the diagram since all nodes, even those holding variables and constants, will be of the same size.

We can eliminate much of the extra space by opting for quite a different strategy: we can represent an n-ary node not by a list of pointers to its operands but by a single pointer to its first operand, with all operands being extended to include a pointer to the next operand of the parent node. Fig. 6.13 illustrates this with respect to $h*(f0+4*f1+f2)/3$.

An appropriate definition of this structure is:

    type *range* $= 1..max$;
        tagtype $= (constant, variable, unary, binary, nary)$;
        narytype $= \uparrow node$;
        node $=$ **record**
                across, down : *narytype*;
                case *tag* : *tagtype* **of**
                constant : (*value* : *real*);
                variable : (*index* : *range*);
                unary : (*unop* : (*neg, recip*));
                binary : (*binop* : (*expon*));
                nary : (*naryop* : (*sum, power*))
                end

Note that this definition obscures the 'n-aryness' of the tree. In

Fig. 6.13. An alternative storage structure for n-ary trees.

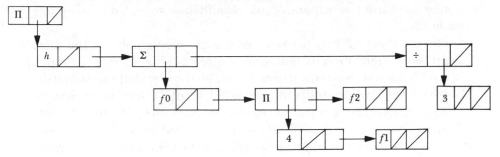

fact, it now has the structure of a binary tree, though a binary tree with a special asymmetric nature. As our choice of identifiers implies, one branch points down the conceptual n-ary tree to a son, the other points across to a brother.

Since this book is not about data structures as such, we leave it to the reader to pursue the use of this form for manipulating expressions.

6.6 Directed graphs

If we allow more than one branch to point to a node, the tree becomes a directed graph, one of the most general structures available. It, too, finds use in the processing of expressions.

Consider the expression $A*r*(1+r)\uparrow n/((1+r)\uparrow n-1)$, which defines the periodic repayment of a mortgage of A, taken out over n periods at a rate of r per period. An n-ary tree for this expression is given on the left of Fig. 6.14. It is a perfectly normal n-ary tree and the function *ExprValue* of Fig. 6.11 can be applied to it. However the

Fig. 6.14. An n-ary tree and a directed graph for $A * r * (1 + r) \uparrow n/((1 + r) \uparrow n - 1)$.

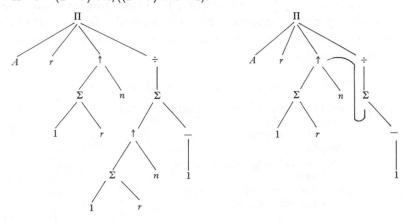

129

subexpression $(1+r){\uparrow}n$ would be evaluated twice, and since the *Power* operation is expensive we would like to avoid this double evaluation.

On the right of Fig. 6.14 we give a directed graph for the same expression. Here there is only one subtree holding $(1+r){\uparrow}n$, though it is on branches from two nodes. Note, by the way that the definition of the *n*-ary tree includes the directed graph. There is no way in Pascal of defining a structure which ensures that all branches are distinct! Note, too, that the *ExprValue* procedure of Fig. 6.11 will operate correctly on a directed graph – but it will cause any common subtree, such as that holding $(1+r){\uparrow}n$, to be evaluated twice.

To ensure a single evaluation we must store more information in the nodes – in particular whether or not the expression represented by the subtree has been already evaluated, and if so what its value is. Thus assuming an array implementation and only a single type of operator node, an appropriate definition is:

```
type range = 1..max;
     tagtype = (constant,variable,operator);
     graphptr = ↑node;
     node = record
               evaluated:Boolean;
               val:real;
               case tag:tagtype of
               constant:(value:real);
               variable:(index:range);
               operator:(op:(neg,recip,sum,prod,expon);
                         nbranches:sizetype;
                         branches:array [sizetype] of graphptr)
            end
```

In Fig. 6.15 we give a procedure for evaluating an expression held in such a graph. It assumes that, for all nodes, *evaluated* is initially false. On completion, the *value* field of all nodes will be set to the appropriate value.

Fig. 6.15. Evaluating an expression held in a graph.

```
function ExprValue(g:graphptr):real;
  var v:real;
      i:sizetype;
  begin
  if not g↑.evaluated then
    begin
    g↑.evaluated := true;
    case g↑.tag of
```

```
constant:g↑.val := g↑.value;
variable:g↑.val := data[g↑.index];
operator:
  begin
  g↑.val := ExprValue(g↑.branch[1]);
  case g↑.op of
  neg:g↑.val := -g↑.val;
  recip:g↑.val := 1/g↑.val;
  sum,prod,expon:
    for i := 2 to g↑.nbranches do
      begin
      v := ExprValue(g↑.branch[i]);
      case g↑.op of
      sum:g↑.val := g↑.val+v;
      prod:g↑.val := g↑.val*v;
      expon:g↑.val := Power(g↑.val,v)
      end { of cases on "g↑.op" }
      end { of loop on "i" }
    end { of cases on "g↑.op" }
    end { of case "operator" }
  end { of cases on "g↑.tag" }
  end { of the evaluation sequence };
ExprValue := g↑.val
end { of function "ExprValue" };
```

Of course, this function, as a side-effect, alters the data structure by changing the *evaluated* field of each node. If we wish to re-evaluate the expression represented by the graph later, as would be the case in an interpreter for example, we would need to restore the graph to its initial state. Fig. 6.16 gives an appropriate procedure.

Fig. 6.16. Resetting all the nodes of a graph.

```
procedure Reset(g:graphptr);
  var i:sizetype;
  begin
  if g↑.evaluated then
    begin
    g↑.evaluated := false;
    if g↑.tag = operator then
      for i := 1 to g↑.nbranches do
        Reset(g↑.branch[i])
    end
  end { of procedure "Reset" };
```

This is a classical procedure which marks each node of the graph. A more familiar form arises when the graph is represented in binary tree form related in an obvious way to that for the n-ary tree described in §6.5.

6.7 Syntax analysis

Searching is perhaps the fundamental operation of computer science; and searching procedures have appeared in many chapters of this book. Almost every data structure can be adapted to its use.

In all the procedures we have written so far, the items are explicitly stored in an array, list or tree, and any structure the items may have is simply ignored. In many situations the items have structure which can be capitalised on by appropriate forms of storage and appropriate searching procedures. We will illustrate this in a progressive manner by starting with the searching of a linked-linear list, as described in Chapter 2.

Suppose we have the usual definition:

> **type** *listptr* = ↑*node*;
>> *node* = **record**
>>> *item* :*itemtype*;
>>> *next* :*listptr*
>>> **end**

We are going to use recursion in a powerful way later on, so we consider now the iterative version of the search procedure, given in Fig. 2.8 and reproduced as Fig. 6.17.

Fig. 6.17. The non-recursive version of *InList*.

```
function InList(l:listptr; k:keytype):Boolean;
  var found:Boolean;
  begin
  found := false;
  while (l <> nil) and not found do
    begin
    found := k = l↑.item.key;
    l := l↑.next
    end;
  InList := found
  end { of function "InList" };
```

Note that this procedure assumes that the key comparison can be done in a single test. We now assume that this is not the case: that is we assume that each item, which we subsequently refer to as

Fig. 6.18. Storage of alternatives and their components.

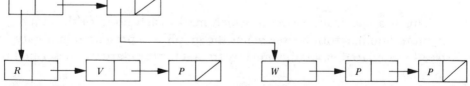

an *alternative* is made up from *components*, which we also store in a list. (Note that the whole item is now the key.)

To take a very simple example, suppose the two alternatives are just *RVP* and *WPP*. Then they would be stored as shown in Fig. 6.18.

An appropriate definition is:

type *comptr* = ↑*compnode*;
          compnode = record
                              comp : *char*;
                              nextcomp : *comptr*
                          end;
          altptr = ↑*altnode*;
          altnode = record
                              alt : *comptr*;
                              nextalt : *altptr*
                          end

The procedure of Fig. 6.17 is easily extended to process this structure by expanding the comparison appropriately. If we assume that the alternative being sought is held in an array of characters which we will call *source*, then the procedure of Fig. 6.19 follows.

Fig. 6.19. Searching alternatives with components.

```
function InList(a:altptr; source:chararray):Boolean;
  var altfound,compfound:Boolean;
      c:comptr;
      s:natural;
  begin
  altfound := false;
  while (a<>nil) and not altfound do
    begin
    s := 1; c := a↑.alt; compfound := true;
    while (c<>nil) and compfound do
      begin
      compfound := c↑.comp = source[s];
      c := c↑.nextcomp; s := s+1
      end;
    altfound := compfound;
    a := a↑.nextalt
    end;
  InList := altfound
  end { of function "InList" };
```

Note that because *s* is reset to 1 for each alternative, the procedure works with a set of alternatives in which some start with the same sequence of components such as:

RVP   RVLL   R1Q

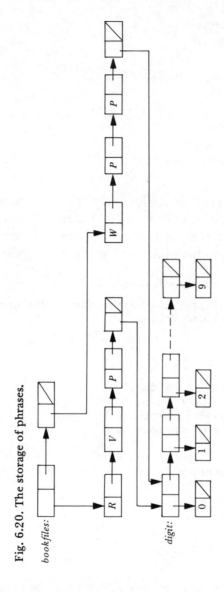

Fig. 6.20. The storage of phrases.

Now let us suppose that the alternatives we are considering are not just *R VP* and *WPP* but:

$$R VP0, R VP1, R VP2, \ldots, R VP9$$
$$WPP0, WPP1, WPP3, \ldots, WPP9$$

We could simply expand our list structure to include all 20 alternatives. However this would ignore the structure of these alternatives, which is that an item consists of either *R VP* or *WPP* followed by a digit. Thus a component can be either a character (as before) or a set of alternatives. We shall call sets of alternatives *phrases*, using a word borrowed from English grammar, and give them names. The name *digit* is appropriate for a phrase describing a digit. For the main phrase we use the name *bookfiles* for reasons which will emerge shortly. Fig. 6.20 gives the appropriate structure, in which we have indicated the substructure associated with each phrase by putting its name on the line containing its alternatives.

The changes to the type definition are trivial: *compnode* now becomes a variant record:

```
tagtype = (compchar,compalt);
compnode = record
              nextcomp : comptr;
              case tag : tagtype of
              compchar : (ch : char);
              compalt : (a : altptr)
           end
```

The changes to *InList* are a little more subtle. Firstly the comparison takes places either directly or by a recursive call depending on the value of *tag*. Secondly, because of the recursion, we need a parameter to specify whereabouts in *source* the process is to start. It will be called as a variable and will always hold the subscript of the next character in *source*. Note that to ensure that the *s* is reset to the 'start' of *source* for each alternative its initial value must be stored in *s0*.

An appropriate procedure is given in Fig. 6.21. Note that we have changed its name to the more appropriate *DefinedBy*:

Fig. 6.21. Searching a structured definition.

```
function DefinedBy(a:altptr; source:chararray;
                        var s:natural):Boolean;
   var altfound,compfound:Boolean;
       c:comptr;
       s0:natural;
```

```
      begin
      s0 := s;
      altfound := false;
      while (a<>nil) and not altfound do
        begin
        s := s0; c := a↑.alt; compfound := true;
        while (c<>nil) and compfound do
          begin
          case c↑.tag of
          compchar:
            begin
            compfound := c↑.ch = source[s];
            s := s+1
            end { of case "compchar" };
          compalt:
            compfound := DefinedBy(c↑.a,source,s)
          end { of cases on "c↑.tag" };
          c := c↑.nextcomp
          end { of looking at components };
        altfound := compfound;
        a := a↑.nextalt
        end;
      DefinedBy := altfound
      end { of function "DefinedBy" };
```

Note that this is one of only two procedures with side-effects in
this book. As we regard it as a step on the way to syntax analysis
we leave it in this form – though with a certain amount of guilt.

The type definitions and the searching function are very general,
and can deal with much more complex situations. For example *RVP*
and *WPP* may be followed by an integer rather than just a digit; and
that in turn followed by a dot and either of the following three-letter
extensions, *PAS*, or *BAK*.

Examples include:

     RVP8.PAS   *RVP11.BAK*   *WPP99.PAS*

but not:

     RVP8.BAS   *RVP11Z.PAS*

As users of the PDP-11 machines may have already recognised these
are all names of files. The initials of the name of this book are *RVP*,
and *WPP* are those of another book. The author's file store contains
many programs for testing the procedures of these books. The test
programs are numbered *RVP0*, *RVP1* and so on. Each exists in two
files: the working file has the extension *PAS* (for Pascal) and the
back-up copy has *BAK*. This file store contains many other files, the
text of projects, answers to assignments and so on. Thus the definition above describes all the files concerned with these books. Fig. 6.22

Fig. 6.22. A phrase structure graph.

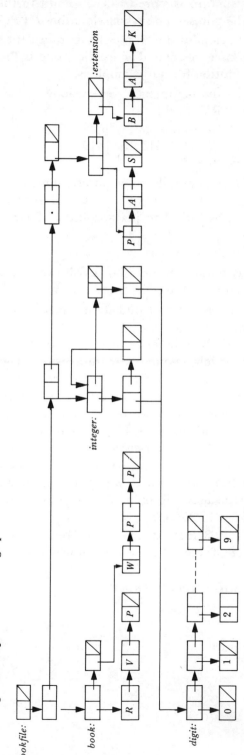

shows how such a structure is stored when, to add further variety, we have introduced the phrase *book* which describes *RVP* and *WPP*.

The English description of these phrases is quite tortuous, and clearly some formalism is needed. The classical one is Backus Naur Form (BNF). The definition for our example is:

⟨bookfile⟩ ::= ⟨book⟩⟨integer⟩.⟨extension⟩
⟨book⟩   ::= RVP|WPP
⟨integer⟩ ::= ⟨digit⟩⟨integer⟩¦⟨digit⟩
⟨digit⟩   ::= 0|1|2|3|4|5|6|7|8|9
⟨extension⟩ ::= PAS|BAK

Here each definition corresponds to a phrase. Phrases are placed within pointed brackets. The symbol ::= is read as 'is defined to be' and the symbol | as 'or'. The juxtaposition of two entities is read as 'followed by'.

Thus the first definition is read as:

'A bookfile is defined to be a book followed by an integer, followed by a dot, followed by an extension.'

The relationship between a set of BNF definitions and the structure graph defined earlier is obvious.

The introduction of BNF immediately suggests syntax analysis. But syntax analysis involves one extra dimension. The function *DefinedBy* is adequate for some purposes. Suppose we want to copy all files defined by *bookfile* onto a floppy disc or distribution (or list them, or delete them). Then we could write a program which scans the file directory and, for each file name in turn, asks whether it is defined by *bookfile*. If so it causes the file to be copied.

In syntax analysis we need to know not merely *whether* a string conforms to a phrase but *why*. That is, we need to know the structure of the string. This is usually represented in a *parse tree*. Fig. 6.23 gives the parse tree for *RVP8.PAS*.

This shows that *RVP8.PAS* is a *bookfile* because it is a *book* followed by an *integer*, followed by a *dot* followed by an *extension*.

Fig. 6.23. The parse tree for *RVP8.PAS*.

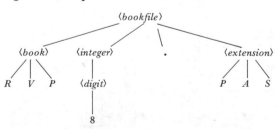

(There is, of course, no other way it could be.) Further, the first three letters are a *book* because they are *R*, *V* and *P* and so on.

This representation, while being easily interpretable by humans is very redundant in that it includes every symbol of *source*. All we really need to know for each phrase is which alternative is involved. Thus, instead of the node marked ⟨*bookfile*⟩ in Fig. 6.23 and its four pointers, we simply record the fact that it is the first (here the only) alternative and three pointers pointing to the nodes for ⟨*book*⟩, ⟨*integer*⟩ and ⟨*extension*⟩. The dot is not explicitly represented. A complete tree is given in Fig. 6.24. To help the reader, the phrase names have been put on the branches. Note that, as we have numbered the alternatives from one, 8 is the ninth.

Fig. 6.24. The succinct form of the parse tree.

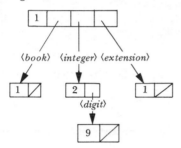

We define the structure of such a parse tree by:

type *parseptr* = ↑*parsenode*;
  parsenode = **record**
        altno : 1..*maxalts*;
        nsubtrees : 0..*maxcomps*;
        subtree : **array** [1..*maxcomps*] **of** *parseptr*
      end

where *maxalts* and *maxcomps* are appropriate constants. In most cases *maxalts* and *maxcomps* are sufficiently small for this array implementation to be viable. In Fig. 6.25 we give a procedure *Parse*, which produces such a tree. More specifically, it parses the string in *source*, starting at *source*[*s*], to see whether it is defined by the definitions in *a*, setting *found* appropriately. If it is, then a parse tree is created which is pointed to by *p*, and *s* is moved over the characters recognised.

Fig. 6.25. A parse procedure.

```
procedure Parse(a:altptr; source:chararray; var found:Boolean;
                var s:natural; var p:parseptr);
   var altfound,compfound:Boolean;
```

139

```
      c:comptr;
      s0:natural;
      altno:1..maxalts;
begin
s0 := s;
altfound := false; altno := 1;
while (a<>nil) and not altfound do
   begin
   new(p); p↑.nsubtrees := 0; p↑.altno := altno;
   s := s0;
   c := a↑.alt;
   compfound := true;
   while (c<>nil) and compfound do
      begin
      case c↑.tag of
      compchar:
         begin
         compfound := c↑.ch = source[s];
         s := s+1;
         end { of case "compchar" };
      compalt:
         begin
         Parse(c↑.a,source,compfound,s,p↑.subtree[p↑.nsubtrees+1]);
         if compfound then
            p↑.nsubtrees := p↑.nsubtrees + 1
         end { of case "compalt" };
      end { of cases on "c↑.tag" };
      c := c↑.nextcomp
      end { of looking at components };
   altfound := compfound;
   if not altfound then { recover }
      begin
      DisposeTree(p);
      a := a↑.nextalt;
      altno := altno+1
      end { of recovery if alternative not found }
   end { of looking at alternatives };
found := altfound
end { of procedure "Parse" };
```

Note the use of *DisposeTree*, whose body is obvious, to return any subtree produced during searching for an alternative which in the end turns out not to be correct.

EXERCISES

6.1 Write a procedure with the heading:
   DisposeBTree(B :Bptr)
   which disposes a B-tree.

6.2 Suppose, as suggested in §6.3, that the items on a B-tree were at all nodes of the B-tree not simply at the leaves. Write appropriate versions of *OnBTree* and *InsertOnBTree*.

6.3 Write a procedure for deleting a key from a B-tree.

6.4 Write a new version of *Tautology* for which the logical expressions are stored in *n*-ary trees.

6.5 Write a differentiation procedure for expressions held in binary trees.

6.6 Rewrite your solutions of Ex. 6.4 and Ex. 6.5 to use directed graphs.

6.7 Write a procedure which, from a set of phrase definitions, produces in an array a random member of the set of strings defined by a specified member of the set of phrases.

7

Simulating nested loops

Of course *n*-ary recursion can occur in the absence of data structures. We illustrate this by transforming a binary procedure, the *Binary Codes* procedure of Fig. 4.27. In Fig. 7.1 we recast it to use a loop.

Fig. 7.1. The procedure *BinaryCodes* using a loop.

```
procedure BinaryCodes(r:range);
  var s:array[range] of 0..1;

  procedure Choose(d:range);
    var i:0..1;
    begin
    for i := 0 to 1 do
      begin
      s[d] := i;
      if d <> r then Choose(d+1) else Process(s,r)
      end { of loop on "i" }
    end { of procedure "Choose" };

  begin
  Choose(1)
  end { of procedure "BinaryCodes" };
```

The procedure is a little slower than the original version but *Process(s)* occurs only once. This might be useful if *Process(s)* were to be replaced in a particular application by an *in situ* sequence rather than a procedure call.

Note that this version of the *BinaryCodes* procedure can be viewed as a simulation of a nest of loops as shown in Fig. 7.2.

Fig. 7.2. The nested loops simulated by *BinaryCodes*.

```
procedure BinaryCodes(r:range);
  var s:array[range] of 0..1;
      i1,i2,...ir:0..1;
```

```
      begin
      for il := 0 to 1 do
        begin
        s[1] := il;
        for i2 := 0 to 1 do
          begin
          s[2] := i2;

                .
               . .
                 .
            for ir := 0 to 1 do
              begin
              s[r] := ir;
              Process(s,r)
              end { of loop on "ir" }

               .
              .
             .

          end   { of loop on "i2" }
        end { of loop on "il" }
      end { of procedure "BinaryCodes" };
```

It goes without saying that if r has a known small value then a nest of loops is probably the best implementation. The virtue of the recursive version is that the simulated nest can be of an unknown size (as here) and can even be of a dynamically varying size.

7.1 The basic algorithm

We now extend our view to consider situations in which the elements of the patterns under consideration are not 0 and 1 but are integers in the same range as the length of the sequence; that is of type *range*.

Thus we are assuming the definitions:

type *range* $= 1..nmax$;
  rangearray = **array** [*range*] **of** *range*

and for subsequent examples:

  rangeset = **set of** *range*;
  rangesetarray = **array** [*range*] **of** *rangeset*

The basic algorithm then generates all patterns of length r whose elements are chosen from the integers 1 to n. Since the order in which the sequences are generated is irrelevant, we will generate them in *lexicographical* order, that is $11\ldots11$, $11\ldots12$, $11\ldots13$, and so on.

In the light of the introduction, the procedure of Fig. 7.3 follows immediately.

Fig. 7.3. The basic procedure.

```
procedure Basic(n,r:range);
  var s:rangearray;

  procedure Choose(d:range);
    var i:range;
    begin
    for i := 1 to n do
      begin
      s[d] := i;
      if d <> r then Choose(d+1) else Process(s,r)
      end { of loop on "i" }
    end { of procedure "Choose" };

  begin
  Choose(1)
  end { of procedure "Basic" };
```

Fig. 7.4 gives the tree of procedure calls, onto the nodes of which we have added the sequence produced in s at the time of the call. It is clearly a generalisation of the tree of Fig. 4.26. Note that, if the statement:

$$\text{if } d <> r \text{ then } Choose(d+1) \text{ else } Process(s,r)$$

of Fig. 7.3 were replaced by the pair of statements:

$$\text{if } d <> r \text{ then } Choose(d+1);$$
$$Process(s,r)$$

then the procedure would produce all sequences of length *up to and including* r. This is often a very useful variant, as is the one in which $Process(s,r)$ comes first.

Note, too, that not all of the loops need to be simulated by calls to *Choose*. If the outer loop were in some way special it could be included within the body of *Basic* itself. We will capitalise on this in some of our examples. Often, too, we can gain some efficiency by using the recursion to simulate pairs of loops.

7.2   Analysis of the basic algorithm

The procedure has two parameters, n and r, and so we seek an analysis in terms of both of them. Thus we require $T_{n,r}$. Note that in all the procedures of this chapter, the parameter d is essentially the same as the recursive depth which is negatively related to the parameter r: as the depth increases, the size of the sub-problem being treated decreases.

Suppose:

   a is the number of operations inside the loop at the bottom level (including those in *Process*),

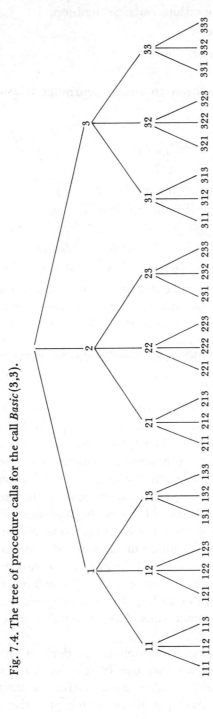

Fig. 7.4. The tree of procedure calls for the call *Basic*(3,3).

145

c is the number of operations inside the loop at other levels,
b is the number of operations outside the loop.

Then from Fig. 7.3 we have

$$T_{n,k} = cn + b + nT_{n,k-1}, \quad k \neq 1$$
$$= an + b, \quad\quad\quad\quad k = 1$$

We can, as usual derive a solution to these recurrence relations by substitution:

$$
\begin{aligned}
T_{n,r} &= cn + b + nT_{n,r-1} \\
&= cn + b + n(cn+b+nT_{n,r-2}) \\
&= cn^2 + (b+c)n + b + n^2 T_{n,r-2} \\
&= cn^2 + (b+c)n + b + n^2(cn+b+nT_{n,r-3}) \\
&= cn^3 + (b+c)n^2 + (b+c)n + b + n^3 T_{n,r-3} \\
&= cn^{r-1} + (b+c)n^{r-2} + \ldots + b + n^{r-1}T_{n,1} \\
&= cn^{r-1} + (b+c)n^{r-2} + \ldots + b + n^{r-1}(an+b) \\
&= an^r + (b+c)n^{r-1} + (b+c)n^{r-2} + \ldots (b+c)n + b
\end{aligned}
$$

Clearly the term an^r dominates except where n is very small indeed. This accords with our intuition that the body of the inner loop of a nest of loops dominates. The coefficient of the second term $(b+c)$ is also in accord with our intuition that operations inside the loop next to the inner loop are of the same significance as those outside the inner loop. (Here the latter consists only of the cost of entry into the inner loop.)

The analysis of a procedure containing an actual nest of loops such as that in Fig. 7.3 (which is possible, of course, only for a fixed k) has the same form. This can be seen by inspection because of its simple structure. If we count fundamental operations, then the coefficient of n^r is $a-1$, the decrement being due to the absence of the test $d=r$ within the inner loop. The coefficient in the recursive version can be reduced to $a-1$ too, at a cost in procedure size, by rephrasing *Choose* so that it contains two loops, one calling itself recursively, and the other performing the actions of *Process*, with an initial test of $d=r$ to determine which loop is to be entered. The test then becomes part of b rather than a and c. We will not do this because, in the applications we consider, the gain in speed is almost negligible, while the loss in space caused by repetition of code is considerable.

Not many problems are general enough to be derived from the basic algorithm (though many authors use it as a basis for solving the n-queens problem). It is generally more useful to start with more constrained algorithms such as those which give rise to the

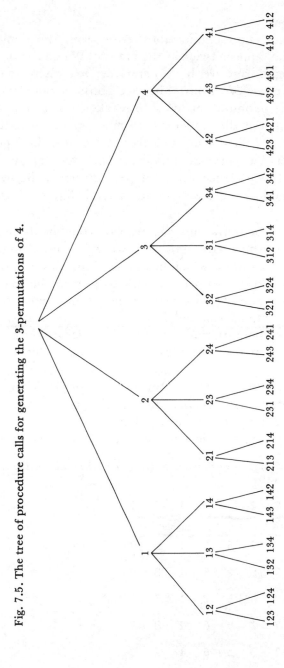

Fig. 7.5. The tree of procedure calls for generating the 3-permutations of 4.

classical combinatorial objects: permutations, combinations, compositions and partitions.

7.3 Permutations

Permutations and combinations arise from the constraint that no number may appear twice in the pattern. Where the order of the elements is significant we have *permutations*; where it is not significant we have *combinations*. First we consider permutations. We will refer to the permutations of 1 to n taken r at a time as the *r-permutations* of n. For the reader whose memory of permutations needs refreshing, Fig. 7.5 gives, at the leaves of the tree, the 3-permutations of 4. When we compare this with the tree for the basic algorithm (Fig. 7.4) we notice that, for permutations, the number of branches per node is constant within a level, but decreases by one at each level.

The generation of permutations has been thoroughly studied and many different algorithms have appeared. We will content ourselves here with just one algorithm, which has some properties that we will want to use later. The reader who wishes to pursue the matter is referred to the paper by Sedgewick (1977) and to the exercises.

Permutation algorithms can be divided into two classes, those which produce the permutations in *pseudo-lexicographical order* and those which do not. By pseudo-lexicographical order we mean that, for all $d < n$, permutations starting with the same d elements are produced consecutively. (This definition includes lexicographical as a special case.) Such permutations are produced as follows:

Suppose a choice has been made for elements 1 to $d-1$. We then make, in turn, all possible choices for the dth element; and for each

Fig. 7.6 The choices for 4th element (ii) given the choice of the first three elements (i).

(i)	3	4	7	2	5	6	1	8	9
		chosen				available			
(ii)	3	4	7	2	5	6	1	8	9
	3	4	7	5	2	6	1	8	9
	3	4	7	6	5	2	1	8	9
	3	4	7	1	5	6	2	8	9
	3	4	7	8	5	6	1	2	9
	3	4	7	9	5	6	1	8	2

such choice, we make, in turn, all possible choices for the $d+1$th element; and so on. This clearly matches the general strategy we are using. The question is: how do we ensure that all possible choices are made for the dth element?

Since the number of choices for the dth element is $n-d+1$, we can store these with the $d-1$ elements chosen so far in the array s, which we initialise to $1, 2, 3 \ldots n$. Assuming $d=4$, $n=9$ and the choice 3 4 7 as the first three elements, we might have the situation of Fig. 7.6(i).

The first choice for the fourth element is already *in situ*; the others appear to its right. They may be put in the correct place in a number of ways. Perhaps the simplest is to interchange each in turn with the fourth as shown in Fig. 7.6(ii). For this to be achieved it is necessary to return to the initial state by re-interchanging at the end of the loop, as shown in the procedure of Fig. 7.7.

Fig. 7.7. A procedure for generating permutations.

```
procedure Perm(n,r:range);
  var s:rangearray;
      i:range;

  procedure Choose(d:range);
    var i,e:range;
    begin
    if d <> r then Choose(d+1) else Process(s,r);
    for i := d + 1 to n do
      begin
      e := s[d]; s[d] := s[i]; s[i] := e;
      if d <> r then Choose(d+1) else Process(s,r);
      e := s[i]; s[i] := s[d]; s[d] := e
      end { of loop on "i" }
    end { of procedure "Choose" };

  begin
  for i := 1 to n do
    s[i] := i;
  Choose(1)
  end { of procedure "Perm" };
```

7.4   Proof of the permutation generating procedure

We made the point in Chapter 1 that recursive procedures are often easy to prove but we have not given any proofs so far, mainly because the proofs are trivial in the sense that the procedures generally implemented, in a direct fashion, the definitions involved. The proofs by induction are obvious.

However, the permutation generator is not quite so obvious, and so we give a proof by way of illustration. It is based on the *inductive hypothesis* that *Choose*(d):

  (i) leaves the values in $s_1 \rightarrow s_{d-1}$ unchanged,
 (ii) causes all the $(r{-}d{+}1)$-permutations of the values in $s_d \rightarrow s_n$ to be produced in $s_d \rightarrow s_r$ in turn,
(iii) returns $s_d \rightarrow s_n$ to its original state.

The proof, like that for the solution of the recurrence relations, is in two parts:

  (*a*) The hypothesis is trivially true for $d{=}r$.
  (*b*) Assume it is true for *Choose*(d+1), then it is true for *Choose*(d) because:

    (i) $s_1 \rightarrow s_{d-1}$ are unchanged as the procedure does not refer to them,
   (ii) all the $(r{-}d{+}1)$-permutations of the value in $s_d \rightarrow s_n$ are produced in $s_d \rightarrow s_r$ because all possible choices are made for s_d, and after each choice, *Choose*(d+1) ensures that the $(r{-}d)$-permutations of the values in $s_{d+1} \rightarrow s_n$ are produced in $s_{d+1} \rightarrow s_r$ in turn,
  (iii) $s_d \rightarrow s_n$ is returned to its original state because *Choose*(d+1) restores $s_{d+1} \rightarrow s_n$ and the final interchange of $s[d]$ and $s[i]$ completes the restoration.

The procedure *Perm* then produces all the r-permutations of the integers 1 to n because it initially places these integers in s and then calls *Choose*(1) which, our induction proof has just shown, causes the r-permutations of the values in $s_1 \rightarrow s_n$ to be produced in $s_1 \rightarrow s_r$.

7.5 An improved permutation generator

We can make two observations about the permutation generator of Fig. 7.7. Firstly, within a call of *Choose*, e always has the same value, the original value of $s[d]$. We can capitalise on this by assigning it before the loop and writing it back afterwards.

The second observation in the procedure has two textual calls both for *Process* and for *Choose*. This can be a disadvantage when the procedure is being used as the basis for some application (such as topological sorting, to be discussed shortly). We will therefore eliminate one of them by simply expanding the loop so that its lower limit is d rather than $d+1$. On the (new) first traverse of the loop $s[d]$ is interchanged with itself giving the same effect (at a small cost) as the original. The modified procedure, which we assume in what follows, is given in Fig. 7.8.

Fig. 7.8. An improved permutation generator.

```
procedure Perm(n,r:range);
  var s:rangearray;
      i:range;

  procedure Choose(d:range);
    var i,e:range;
    begin
    e := s[d];
    for i := d to n do
      begin
      s[d] := s[i]; s[i] := e;
      if d <> r then Choose(d+1) else Process(s,r);
      s[i] := s[d]
      end { of loop on "i" };
    s[d] := e
    end { of procedure "Choose" };

  begin
  for i := 1 to n do
    s[i] := i;
  Choose(1)
  end { of procedure "Perm" };
```

7.6 Analysis of the permutation generator

The analysis of this procedure follows along the same lines as that of the basic procedure, though it is a little more complex. If we use the same conventions:

    a is the number of operations inside the loop at the bottom level,

    c is the number of operations inside the loop at other levels,

    b is the number of operations outside the loop,

then we have:

$$T_{n,k} = cn + b + nT_{n-1,k-1}, \quad k \neq 1$$
$$= an + b, \qquad\qquad\qquad k=1$$

If we use the notation $[^n_r]$ for the r-term product $n(n-1)(n-2)\ldots(n-r+1)$ then the solution of these equations is:

$$T_{n,r} = a[^n_r] + (b+c)\,[^{\,n}_{r-1}] + (b+c)\,[^{\,n}_{r-2}] + \ldots + b$$

Rather than derive this solution (by substitution) we prove it, as usual in two parts:

(i) $T_{n,1} = a[^n_1] + b$
       $= an + b$

(ii) $T_{n,r} = cn + b + nT_{n-1,r-1}$

$$cn + b + n\{a[\begin{smallmatrix}n-1\\r-1\end{smallmatrix}] + (b+c)[\begin{smallmatrix}n-1\\r-2\end{smallmatrix}] + \ldots + b\}$$

$$cn + b + a[\begin{smallmatrix}n\\r\end{smallmatrix}] + (b+c)[\begin{smallmatrix}n\\r-1\end{smallmatrix}] + \ldots + bn$$

$$a[\begin{smallmatrix}n\\r\end{smallmatrix}] + (b+c)[\begin{smallmatrix}n\\r-1\end{smallmatrix}] + (b+c)[\begin{smallmatrix}n\\r-1\end{smallmatrix}] + \ldots + (b+c)n + b$$

Again this accords with our intuition if we relate the solution to the tree of Fig. 7.5. We see there are $[\begin{smallmatrix}n\\r\end{smallmatrix}]$ leaves, each corresponding to a permutation and each implying a cost of a due to the traverse of the inner loop. Immediately above the leaves are $[\begin{smallmatrix}n\\r-1\end{smallmatrix}]$ nodes each implying a cost of b for the instructions outside the inner loop plus c for the instructions of a traverse of the loop next to the inner loop, and so on.

It is interesting to compare the form of the solution with that of the basic algorithm.

$$T_{n,r} = an^r + (b+c)n^{r-1} + (b+c)n^{r-2} + \ldots + (b+c)n + b$$

The first term dominates, but less than it did with the basic algorithm, since as $r \to n$ the other terms increase in weight. For example, if we are generating the n-permutations of n, we have $r = n-1$ (since the choice of the $n-1$ elements automatically causes the nth to be in place), then the cost becomes

$$T_n = an! + (b+c)\frac{n!}{2} + \ldots$$

so that the second term has half the weight of the first.

7.7 An application: topological sorting

Consider the *directed acyclic graph* of Fig. 7.9(i), taken from Wirth (1976).

If we think of the arrow on the arc between two nodes as indicating that the node at its tail is, in some sense, the predecessor of the node at its head, then a topological sort is an arrangement of the nodes such that if node i precedes node j (in the above sense) then i will precede j in the listing. As Fig. 7.9(ii) confirms 7 9 1 2 4 6 3 5 8 10 is one such sort. If the nodes are numbered consecutively from 1, that is if they are of type *range*, then a topological sort is a permutation subject to the precedence condition. We can base a solution on the permutation generator of Fig. 7.9.

The graph can be defined by the number of its nodes and, for each node, the set of nodes which must precede it. Thus:

Fig. 7.9. A directed acyclic graph (i) and its linearised version (ii).

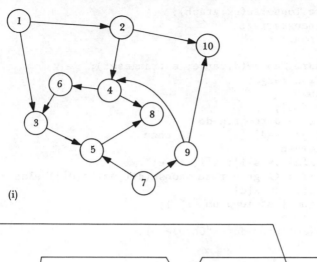

(i)

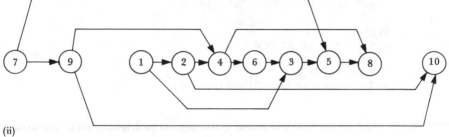

(ii)

```
type graph = record
             n : range;
             pred : rangesetarray
             end
```

where *rangesetarray* was defined earlier as:

```
rangeset = set of range;
rangesetarray = array [range] of rangeset
```

To determine more efficiently whether the predecessors of any element have already been chosen, we keep the current choice of the first d elements, not only in the array s but also in a set ss, of the type *rangeset*. Fig. 7.10 gives a procedure, in which the set ss is transmitted as a parameter. We often use this technique. The alternative is to make ss local to the outer procedure, to have it incremented before the recursive call, and to have it decremented after the call.

153

Fig. 7.10. A procedure for generating topological sorts.

```
procedure Topsorts(gr:graph);
  var s:rangearray;
      i:range;

  procedure Choose(d:range; ss:rangeset);
    var i,e:range;
    begin
    e := s[d];
    for i := d to gr.n do
      if gr.pred[s[i]] <= ss then
        begin
        s[d] := s[i]; s[i] := e;
        if d <> gr.n then Choose(d+1,ss+[s[d]]) else Process(s,d
        s[i] := s[d]
        end { of loop on "i" };
    s[d] := e
    end { of procedure "Choose" };

  begin
  for i := 1 to gr.n do
    s[i] := i;
  Choose(1,[])
  end { of procedure "Topsorts" };
```

Note that if we had wanted only one topological sort, we could have trivially transformed *TopSorts* by including with *Process(s)* a goto-statement, and labelling the end of the (outer) procedure. We used a similar technique in Chapter 5 with the function *Tautology*, where we noted that this was an important use of a goto-statement.

7.8 Combinations

We noted in §7.4 that the difference between permutations and combinations is that in permutations the order of the elements is significant. Since the order of the generation of the combinations and the order of the elements within the combination do not matter, we are free to choose an order to suit our tastes. Our algorithm will produce the combinations in lexicographical order as in Fig. 7.11.

This particular choice of ordering naturally places a lower bound on what can be chosen as the dth element. It is one more than the current choice of the $(d-1)$th element. The upper bound is easily seen to be the choice that leaves one choice for each of the subsequent elements. This is $n-r+d$.

Fig. 7.12 gives an appropriate procedure in which the lower bound is transmitted as a parameter. This enables the general mechanism to be used for $d=1$ as well.

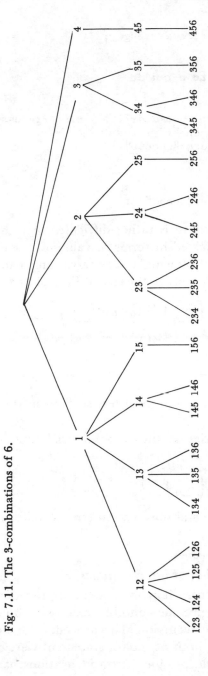

Fig. 7.11. The 3-combinations of 6.

Fig. 7.12. A procedure for generating the r-combinations of n.

```
procedure Combs(n,r:range);
  var s:rangearray;

  procedure Choose(d,lower:range);
    var i:range;
    begin
    for i := lower to n-r+d do
      begin
      s[d] := i;
      if d <> r then Choose(d+1,i+1) else Process(s,r)
      end { of loop on "i" }
    end { of procedure "Choose" };

  begin
  Choose(1,1)
  end { of procedure "Combs" };
```

The analysis of the procedure is rather difficult, since the recurrence relations must be expressed in terms of values of the elements currently chosen. However, following the observations made about permutations we can appeal directly to the tree of Fig. 7.11 to deduce:

$$T_{n,r} = a \binom{n}{r} + (b+c)\binom{n-1}{r-1} + (b+c)\binom{n-2}{r-2}$$
$$+ \ldots + (b+c)(n-r+1) + b$$

where $\binom{n}{r}$ is equal to $\dfrac{n!}{r!\,(n-r)!}$.

Again the first term dominates, but even less so than in the case of permutations.

Using elementary properties of the combinatorial function, this can be rewritten:

$$T_{n,r} = a \binom{n}{r} + (b+c)\binom{n}{r-1} - c$$

which leads us to a more general observation (true of all the procedures in this chapter) that:

$$T_{n,r} = a \times number\ of\ leaves$$
$$+ (b+c) \times number\ of\ internal\ nodes + b$$

We have emphasized how easy it is to write poor procedures. The generation of combinations provides another example, though it is not strictly due to the use of recursion. The procedure of Fig. 7.12 would still work if the upper limit of the for-statement were changed from $n-r+d$ to n. This would produce extra invocations of *Choose* which would not lead to combinations because at some level *lower* would be greater than n, and so the loop would act as a null statement. As a result, the time would be given by:

$$T_{n,r} = a \binom{n}{r} + (b+c) \binom{n}{r-1} + (b+c) \binom{n}{r-2}$$
$$+ \ldots + (b+c)n + b$$

7.9   Subsets

Of course, if we want not simply the r-combinations of n, but all the 1-combinations, 2-combinations, . . . and r-combinations, we must relax the upper limit to n. Since the elements of a combination are distinct, and no order is implied amongst the elements, a combination can be thought of as a subset. Because of the example we are going to use, we will do so. Fig. 7.13 gives a procedure for generating all the subsets of a set of n elements.

Fig. 7.13. A procedure for generating subsets of a set.

```
procedure Subsets(n:range);

  procedure Choose(lower:range; s:rangeset);
    var i:range;
    begin
    for i := lower to n do
      begin
      Process(s+[i]);
      if lower <> n then Choose(i+1,s+[i])
      end { of loop on "i" }
    end { of procedure "Choose" };

  begin
  Choose(1,[])
  end { of procedure "Subsets" };
```

If we compare this procedure with the *Combs* procedure of Fig. 7.12 we notice an important difference: s, which is now of type *rangeset*, is not a variable of the outer procedure but instead is transmitted as a parameter of *Choose* (and therefore d is no longer relevant). This relies on the set facilities of Pascal. If those were not available, and sets had to be simulated by arrays, we would have to revert to the other form.

7.10   An application: the set covering problem (SCP)

Suppose we have a family (f) of m subsets $b_1, b_2, \ldots, b_m$ of a given set, each with an associated cost $c_1, c_2 \ldots, c_m$. The set covering problem (SCP), is to find that selection of subsets in f that covers the given set (i.e. the union of the subsets of the selection is the given set) and which, of all those that cover the set, has the smallest cost.

An appropriate data structure might be:

```
type family = record
                m :natural;
                n :range;
                member :array [range] of
                        record
                        b :rangeset;
                        c :real
                        end

              end
```

Note that this requires us to produce not all selections that cover the given set but the optimal one.

Thus the actual processing takes place in the outer procedure. Within the inner procedure, where previously we processed, we now update the best solution so far found.

Fig. 7.14 gives a procedure in which s represents the selection of f currently generated and *uncovered* represents those elements of the original set not covered by s. As we expand s it is worth including a new member, b_i say, only if b_i includes some elements not yet covered and if the total cost of the selection including b_i is less than that of the best set so far found.

Fig. 7.14. A procedure for the set-covering problem.

```
procedure SCP(f:family);
  var bestset:rangeset;
      bestcost:real;

    procedure Choose(lower:range; s,uncovered:rangeset; partcost:real);
      var i:range;
      begin
      for i := lower to f.m do
        with f.member[i] do
          begin
          if (b*uncovered <> []) and (partcost+c < bestcost) then
            begin
            if b >= uncovered then
              begin
              bestcost := partcost + c;
              bestset := s + [i]
              end
            else if i <> f.m then
              Choose(i+1,s+[i],uncovered-b,partcost+c)
            end
          end
      end { of procedure "Choose" };
```

158

```
begin
bestcost := maxint;
Choose(1,[],[1..f.n],0);
Process(bestset,f.m,bestcost)
end { of procedure "SCP" };
```

7.11   Compositions and partitions

If we now return to the basic algorithm and apply the constraint that the elements should sum to n (while allowing the elements to be repeated) we get *compositions* (if the order is important) and *partitions* (if it is not). Applications may add further constraints, of course, such as restricting the number of elements or their size. We consider here only compositions leaving partitions as an exercise.

Fig. 7.15 gives the tree for the generation of the compositions of 5.

Fig. 7.15. The compositions of 5.

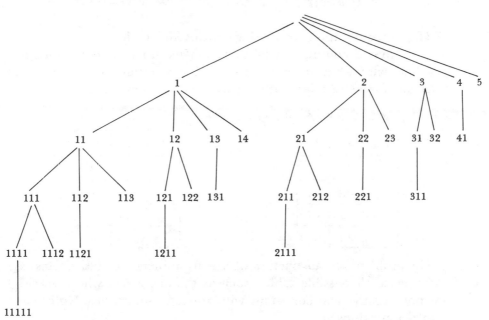

A procedure can be easily produced from the basic procedure of Fig. 7.3 as shown in Fig. 7.16. No comment is needed except to say that the parameter *residue* holds that part of n which is still available for subsequent elements.

Fig. 7.16. A procedure for generating compositions of n.

```
procedure Comp(n:range);
    var s:rangearray;
```

```
procedure Choose(d,residue:range);
  var i:range;
  begin
  for i := 1 to residue do
    begin
    s[d] := i;
    if i = residue then Process(s,d)
    else Choose(d+1,residue-i)
    end { of loop on "i" }
  end { of procedure "Choose" };

begin
Choose(1,n)
end { of procedure "Comp" };
```

For the analysis we again resort to the tree and to some of the basic properties of compositions to arrive at:

$$T_n = a2^{n-1} + (b+c)(2^{n-1}-1) + b$$
$$= (a+b+c)2^{n-1} - c$$

7.12 An application: generating contingency tables

An $n \times 2$ contingency table is a matrix of n rows and 2 columns together with what are called row and sum totals. Fig. 7.17 gives a schema for a 4×2 table, together with an actual example.

Fig. 7.17. A 4×2 contingency table.

A_{11}	A_{12}	R_1
A_{21}	A_{22}	R_2
A_{31}	A_{32}	R_3
A_{41}	A_{42}	R_4
C_1	C_2	

3	1	4
1	0	1
2	0	2
1	2	3
7	3	

The problem (an abstraction of a real problem for statisticians) is to generate all possible tables, such as the one given, whose entries are non-negative and consistent with row and sum totals. Note that 0 entries are allowed.

Clearly we need consider only the first column, since the choice of any element in that column, say A_{i1} automatically specifies the corresponding element in the second column A_{i2}, their sum being R_i. The elements of the column form a composition of C_1, subject to the constraint that it is of length n. The elements themselves have tighter constraints than this. To see why, we consider Fig. 7.17 again. A choice of $A_{11} = 0$ would immediately be invalid since it implies that $A_{12} = 4$ which in turn implies that some other element A_{i2}

would have to be negative to satisfy C_2. The bounds for a given element are, of course, dependent on the current choices of the previous elements and, for the dth element, are given by:

$$lower_d = max \begin{cases} R_d - \left(C_2 - \sum_{i=1}^{d-1} A_{i,2}\right) \\ 0 \end{cases}$$

$$= max \begin{cases} R_d - residue\ of\ C_2 \\ 0 \end{cases}$$

$$upper_d = min \begin{cases} C_1 - \sum_{i=1}^{d-1} A_{i,1} \\ R_d \end{cases}$$

$$= min \begin{cases} residue\ of\ C_1 \\ R_d \end{cases}$$

Let us assume the following definitions:

```
type val = 0..vmax;
     size = 1..smax;
     table = record
               n:size;
               a:array [size,1..2] of val;
               r:array [size] of val;
               c1,c2:val
             end
```

The procedure of Fig. 7.18 follows.

Fig. 7.18. A procedure for $n \times 2$ contingency tables.

```
procedure Contingency2(t:table);

    procedure Choose(d:size; res1,res2:val);
      var i,lower,upper:val;
      begin
      with t do
        begin
        if r[d]>res2 then lower := r[d]-res2 else lower := 0;
        if r[d]<res1 then upper := r[d] else upper := res1;
        for i := lower to upper do
          begin
          a[d,1] := i;
          a[d,2] := r[d]-i;
          if d = n then Process(t)
          else Choose(d+1,res1-i,res2-a[d,2])
          end { of loop on "i" }
        end { of with "t" }
      end { of procedure "Choose" };

    begin
    Choose(1,t.c1,t.c2)
    end { of procedure "Contingency2" };
```

161

7.13   An example of double recursion: Latin squares

Of course double recursion occurs in these combinatorial problems too. We give an example here in which the two instances of recursion merge together. A Latin square of order n is a square of size $n \times n$ in which the numbers 1 to n appear once in each row and once in each column. Examples of squares of order n are given in Fig. 7.19.

Fig. 7.19 Some Latin squares of order 4.

```
1 2 3 4        2 4 1 3        1 2 3 4
2 3 4 1        3 1 2 4        2 1 4 3
3 4 1 2        4 2 3 1        3 4 1 2
4 1 2 3        1 3 4 2        4 3 2 1
```

We could regard a square as a sequence of n^2 elements, the elements being selected from the integers 1 to n, and adapt the basic combinatorial algorithm accordingly. However the constraints on the sequence are complex: they are the constraints corresponding to the fact that each row and each column consists of a permutation of the integers 1 to n.

It seems preferable to recognise explicitly the two-dimensional nature of the problem and the fact that it is essentially about permutations. Thus we can adapt the permutation generator of Fig. 7.8. In terms of that procedure, after we have generated a row, instead of processing it we have to create the next row (unless it is the last, in which case we do the processing). Thus we need recursion to organise the creation of the rows in turn as well as the creation of an individual row. Clearly *Choose* can be used for both tasks provided we give it an extra parameter to indicate which row is being chosen. To highlight this we use the identifiers *row* and *col* for these parameters.

Of course, the permutations chosen for each row are restricted by the constraint that the columns must also be permutations. To satisfy this constraint, we keep for each column the set of elements so far chosen for that column. An element is a valid choice for a given column only if it does not appear in that column's set. These elements are held in an array *ss* of the type *rangesetarray*:

type *rangeset* = **set of** *range*;
     rangesetarray = **array** [*range*] **of** *rangeset*

An appropriate procedure is given in Fig. 7.20.

Fig. 7.20. A procedure for generating Latin squares.

```
procedure LatinSquare(n:range);
  var s:array[range,range] of range;
      ss:rangesetarray;
      row,col:range;

  procedure Choose(row,col:range);
    var e1,e2,i:range;
    begin
    el := s[row,col];
    for i := col to n do
      begin
      e2 := s[row,i];
      if not (e2 in ss[col]) then
        begin
        s[row,col] := e2; s[row,i] := el;
        ss[col] := ss[col] + [e2];
        if col <> n then Choose(row,col+1)
        else if row <> n then Choose(row+1,1) else Process(s,n);
        s[row,i] := e2;
        ss[col] := ss[col] - [e2]
        end
      end { of loop on "i" };
    s[row,col] := el
    end { of procedure "Choose" };

  begin
  for col := 1 to n do
    begin
    for row := 1 to n do
      s[row,col] := col;
    ss[col] := []
    end { of loop on "col" };
  Choose(1,1)
  end { of procedure "LatinSquare" };
```

7.14 Approaching combinatorial problems

It is clear from the previous sections of this chapter that combinatorial problems by their very nature are time-consuming. Where no special purpose algorithms exist we simply have to use the exhaustive search procedure given here. Two guidelines are helpful though.

First, use the thinnest tree. That is, use combinations in preference to permutations and permutations in preference to the basic algorithm; using partitions in preference to compositions and compositions in preference to the basic algorithm. This avoids the production of duplicate solutions which, somehow or other, would have to be eliminated.

Second, prune as hard as possible. That is, the sooner the branch of a tree can be eliminated (because it will not lead to any solution) the better. Often as we have seen, this leads to determining more closely the bounds on the values each element may take.

EXERCISES

7.1 Write a procedure that will print out all the n-digit numbers that are equal to the sum of the nth power of their digits. (For example, if $n=3$, then it will print 153, 370 and 371.)

7.2 Write a permutation generator that produces them in lexicographical order. Suppose, as in Fig. 7.6, that $d=4$, $n=9$, and that the current choice for the first three elements is 347. The situation is as shown in Fig. 7.21(i), and the results of the choice of the fourth element are shown in Fig. 7.21(ii).

Fig. 7.21 Choices for a lexicographic permutation generation.

(i) 3	4	7	1	2	5	6	8	9	
	chosen			available					
(ii) 3	4	7	1	2	5	6	8	9	
3	4	7	2	1	5	6	8	9	
3	4	7	5	1	2	6	8	9	
3	4	7	6	1	2	5	8	9	
3	4	7	8	1	2	5	6	9	
3	4	7	9	1	2	5	6	8	

7.3 Consider the permutation procedures of Fig. 7.7 and Fig. 7.8. Determine the values of a, b and c in terms of fundamental operations. Using the expressions derived in §7.6 for $T_{n,r}$, determine quantitatively the benefit of the improvement.

7.4 Write a procedure based on the permutation generator of Fig. 7.7 to solve the n-queens problem. That is, determine the ways in which n queens may be placed on an $n \times n$ chessboard in such a way that no queen is under attack from any other. (If the rows and columns are numbered from 1 to n, then we can represent a solution by the sequence q, where

q_i, $i=1\ldots n$, is the column in which the queen on row q is placed. Clearly q is an n-permutation of n.)

7.5 Consider a graph such as the one in Fig. 7.22. A *clique* of a graph is a set of nodes of the graph each of which is joined

Fig. 7.22. An arbitrary graph.

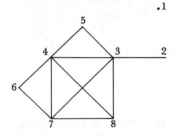

to all the others. Further, this set of nodes must not be included in some other (larger) clique. Thus the cliques of the graph of Fig. 7.22 are:

{1}
{2, 3}
{3, 4, 5}
{4, 6, 7}
{3, 4, 7, 8}

Clearly the cliques are subsets of the set of nodes. Write a procedure for generating the cliques of a graph.

7.6 A race track for model cars can be made from straight pieces of length l and quadrant pieces of radius l. Fig. 7.23 shows a track made from six straights and four curves. Assuming

Fig. 7.23. A race-track with six straights and four curves.

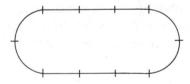

that arrangements can be made for crossovers, write a procedure that will generate all distinct track layout given s straights and c curves.

7.7 Write a procedure for generating partitions.

7.8 Extend the contingency table generator of Fig. 7.18 to deal with $n \times m$ tables.

8
The elimination of recursion

We are going to finish our study of recursion in Pascal programming by seeing how to eliminate it. This may seem a curious thing to do given that for seven chapters we have strongly pressed the case for using recursion, but there are a number of reasons for doing so.

Firstly, it may be that the system we are using does not allow recursion. Such a restriction will not arise with Pascal, of course, but sometimes we are obliged to write in Fortran where such a restriction is part of the language definition. If we can translate a recursive procedure into a non-recursive one, then we can still retain the advantages of *designing* our programs recursively.

Secondly, where there are two or more forms of recursion in a procedure, its readability may be improved by the removal of one of the recursive aspects. We discussed this idea in Chapter 2 and used it in Chapters 5 and 6. For improved readability, the recursion to be eliminated must be of the preorder, linear type.

Thirdly, we may have tight space constraints or very tight time constraints and it may be that the replacement of a recursive procedure by an iterative one allows us to satisfy those constraints.

Finally, and most importantly, we may wish to consider the elimination of recursion purely to increase our understanding of recursive procedures.

8.1 The tail recursion rule

There is one simple rule that everybody knows. It relates to preorder procedures (those with tail recursion) though we express it in the informal terms usually used: if the last statement of a procedure is a (directly) recursive call, replace it by statements to reassign the parameters and to jump to the first statement. Consider, for example, the procedure *WriteList* of Fig. 2.2 which is reproduced as Fig. 8.1.

Fig. 8.1. The recursive version of *WriteList*.

```
procedure WriteList(l:listptr);
  begin
  if l <> nil then
    begin
    WriteItem(l↑.item);
    WriteList(l↑.next)
    end
  end { of procedure "WriteList" };
```

It can be recast as shown in Fig. 8.2.

Fig. 8.2. A non-recursive version of *WriteList*.

```
procedure WriteList(l:listptr);
  label 1;
  begin
1:if l <> nil then
    begin
    WriteItem(l↑.item);
    l := l↑.next;
    goto 1
    end
  end { of procedure "WriteList" };
```

It is trivial to recast this in the structured form of Fig. 8.3.

Fig. 8.3. A structured version of *WriteList*.

```
procedure WriteList(l:listptr);
  begin
  while l <> nil do
    begin
    WriteItem(l↑.item);
    l := l↑.next
    end
  end { of procedure "WriteList" };
```

This rule is quite general in that it applies not only to linear recursive procedures such as *WriteList*, but to binary and *n*-ary procedures as well. Only in the linear case, however, is the recursion completely removed. All the cases in the earlier chapters where we used iteration instead of recursion were of this type.

On the other hand, the rule is quite restrictive in that it does not apply to postorder procedures; nor does it apply to those preorder procedures in which any parameter called as a variable is changed on each recursive call. One example of this latter class is the procedure *CopyList* of Fig. 2.3. Consequently we will consider this rule no further, regarding it as a simple consequence of the more general techniques to be discussed.

Recursion elimination is currently the subject of a great deal of research and it would require a whole book to do it justice. What we will do therefore is consider just three techniques which have a fairly wide applicability. We will illustrate each with respect to a general linear schema, Fig. 8.4, which includes the preorder and postorder schemata of Chapter 2. We will, of course, touch on other aspects.

Fig. 8.4. A general linear recursive schema.

```
procedure C(x:xtype);
  begin
  if P(x) then M(x)
  else
    begin
    S1(x);
    C(F(x));
    S2(x)
    end
  end { of procedure "C" };
```

We assume that all the components of x are changed in each call (as is usually the case in this book). If this is not true then the techniques used here will sometimes produce redundant assignments, though these are easily eliminated. Further we assume that x consists of value parameters only, a point we will return to in §8.5.

8.2 Direct simulation of the stack

The standard method of conversion is to simulate the stack of all the previous activation records by a local stack. Thus:

(i) The call $C(x)$ is replaced by a sequence to:
  (a) push x onto the stack,
  (b) set the new value of x,
  (c) jump to the start of the procedure.
(ii) At the end of the procedure a sequence is added which:
  (a) tests whether the stack is empty, and ends if it is, otherwise
  (b) pops x from the stack,
  (c) jumps to the statement after the sequence replacing the call.

Fig. 8.5 illustrates this with respect to the general schema of Fig. 8.4.

Fig. 8.5. An unstructured non-recursive schema.

```
procedure C(x:xtype);
  label 1,2;
  var s:stack of xtype;
  begin
  clear s;
1:if P(x) then M(x)
  else
    begin
    S1(x);
    push x onto s;
    x := F(x);
    goto 1;
  2:S2(x)
    end;
  if s not empty then
    begin
    pop x from s;
    goto 2
    end
  end { of procedure "C" };
```

Note that the simulation by *s* of the activation record stack achieves some efficiency since it avoids the stacking of:

(i) the stack link (because there is only one activation record),

(ii) the return address link (because there is only one call).

It is a relatively simple matter to recast this in the structured form of Fig. 8.6.

Fig. 8.6. The structured non-recursive schema.

```
procedure C(x:xtype);
  var s:stack of xtype;
  begin
  clear s;
  while not P(x) do
    begin
    S1(x);
    push x onto s;
    x := F(x)
    end;
  M(x);
  while s not empty do
    begin
    pop x from s;
    S2(x)
    end
  end { of procedure "C" };
```

We consider now the application of this schema to the procedure *WriteNatural* first given in Fig. 1.5 and reproduced in Fig. 8.7.

Fig. 8.7. The *WriteNatural* procedure.

```
procedure WriteNatural(i:natural);
  begin
  if i < 10 then
    write(chr(i+ord('0')))
  else
    begin
    WriteNatural(i div 10);
    write(chr(i mod 10 + ord('0')))
    end
  end { of procedure "WriteNatural" };
```

The result is given in Fig. 8.8: it is precisely that of Fig. 1.7.

Fig. 8.8. A non-recursive version of *WriteNatural.*

```
procedure WriteNatural(i:natural);
  var s:stack of natural;
  begin
  clear s;
  while i >= 10 do
    begin
    push i onto s;
    i := i div 10
    end;
  write(chr(i+ord('0')));
  while s not empty do
    begin
    pop i from s;
    write(chr(i mod 10 + ord('0')))
    end
  end { of procedure "WriteNatural" };
```

It is clear that the schema when applied to *WriteList* will produce a procedure that is more complex and less efficient than the one produced by the tail recursion rule of §8.1. Let us then return to the schema, Fig. 8.6, and see what simplifications arise if the procedure is preorder, that is if $S2(x)$ is null.

Let us look at the second loop. If $S2(x)$ is null then the loop merely pops values of x and does nothing with them. Clearly, we can eliminate the popping, if we can stop the loop cycling indefinitely. But as the loop is now null, we can do even better: we can eliminate it entirely!

Now to the first loop. Since we do not pop values of x, there is no point pushing them. Indeed there is no point having a stack at all. Thus we are led to the schema of Fig. 8.9.

Fig. 8.9. A non-recursive preorder schema.

```
procedure C(x:xtype);
  begin
  while not P(x) do
    begin
    S1(x);
    x := F(x)
    end;
  M(x)
  end { of procedure "C" };
```

It is clear that when we apply this schema to *WriteList* we get the optimal procedure of Fig. 8.3.

This standard method of recursion elimination is very powerful, since it mimics precisely the action that the run-time system takes for the implementation of recursion. However, it produces very unstructured programs. Rather than consider its application to binary and *n*-ary recursion in general, we simply show it in action in quite a complex case. Consider Ackermann's function of Fig. 5.16, which is reproduced as Fig. 8.10.

Fig. 8.10. Ackermann's function.

```
function Ack(m,n:natural):natural;
  begin
  if m = 0 then Ack := n+1
  else if n = 0 then Ack := Ack(m-1,1)
  else Ack := Ack(m-1,Ack(m,n-1))
  end { of function "Ack" };
```

We first express it as a procedure, Fig. 8.11.

Fig. 8.11. Ackermann's procedure.

```
procedure CalcAck(var Ack:natural; m,n:natural);
  begin
  if m = 0 then Ack := n+1
  else if n = 0 then CalcAck(Ack,m-1,1)
  else
    begin
    CalcAck(Ack,m,n-1);
    CalcAck(Ack,m-1,Ack)
    end
  end { of procedure "CalcAck" };
```

When we apply the standard technique we arrive at the procedure of Fig. 8.12, in which we have taken a few (obvious) liberties with Pascal. Note in particular the use of pointed brackets to surround the denotations of the fields of a record.

171

Fig. 8.12. A non-recursive version of Ackermann's procedure.

```
procedure CalcAck(var Ack:natural; m,n:natural);
  label 1,2,3,4;
  var s:stack of <natural,natural,1..4>;
      l:1..4;
  begin
  clear s;
1:if m = 0 then Ack := n + 1
  else if n = 0 then
    begin
    push <m,n,2> onto s;
    m := m-1;
    n := 1;
    goto 1;
    2:end
  else
    begin
    push <m,n,3> onto s;
    n := n-1;
    goto 1;
    3:push <m,n,4> onto s;
    m := m-1;
    n := Ack;
    goto 1;
    4:end;
  if s not empty then
    begin
    pop <m,n,l> from s;
    case l of
    1:goto 1;
    2:goto 2;
    3:goto 3;
    4:goto 4
    end { of cases on "l" }
    end
  end { of procedure "CalcAck" };
```

The advantages of this classical technique are that it is easy to implement and that it is completely general. However, it produces unstructured code which is hard to restructure; and it provides no insight into the program transformation problem.

8.3 Direct use of the stack.

It is clear that all recursive procedures, except linear preorder ones, require a stack if the recursion is to be eliminated. The second technique we consider recognises this fact directly by using the stack to hold future obligations.†

† The idea is due to Knuth (1974).

Consider the linear schema of Fig. 8.4 again. A call for this procedure $C(x)$, can be regarded as an obligation to perform $C(x)$ and so s is initialised accordingly. The body of the procedure consists of a loop in which an obligation is popped off the stack and then honoured. A stack element will consist of a value of x and an indication of the nature of the obligation. We use the type:

$$\text{type } obligation = (CFx, S1x, S2x)$$

If the obligation is a call, then to honour this we test $P(x)$. If it is true we obey $M(x)$ otherwise we stack the three obligations implied in $S1(x)$; $C(F1(x))$; $S2(x)$, in reverse order of course. To honour the obligation $S1x$, we simply perform $S1(x)$; to honour $S2x$, we perform $S2(x)$.

If we implement this literally we arrive at the procedure of Fig. 8.13.

Fig. 8.13. An obvious linear schema using obligations.

```
procedure C(x:xtype);
  type obligation = (CFx,S1x,S2x);
  var oblig:obligation;
      s:stack of <xtype,obligation>;
  begin
  clear s;
  push <x,CFx> onto s;
  repeat
    pop <x,oblig> from s;
    case oblig of
    S1x:S1(x);
    S2x:S2(x);
    CFx:if P(x) then M(x)
          else
            begin
            push <x,S2x> onto s;
            push <F(x),CFx> onto s;
            push <x,S1x> onto s
            end { of case "CFx" }
    end { of cases on "oblig" }
  until s empty
  end { of procedure "C" };
```

We can improve this procedure in two stages. We first note:

(i) There is no point pushing $\langle x, S1x \rangle$ onto s since we immediately (on the next traverse of the loop) pop it, and perform $S1(x)$. We can instead simply perform $S1(x)$, and $S1x$ can be eliminated as an obligation.

(ii) This performance of $S1(x)$ can take place before the remaining pushes.

(iii) There is no point pushing $\langle F(x), CFx \rangle$ onto s (it is now the last statement of the CFx obligation) and immediately popping it. The whole CFx obligation can be written as a loop.

The result is shown in Fig. 8.14.

Fig. 8.14. A better linear schema using obligations.

```
procedure C(x:xtype);
  type obligation = (CFx,S2x);
  var oblig:obligation;
      s:stack of <xtype,obligation>;
  begin
  clear s;
  push <x,CFx> onto s;
  repeat
    pop <x,oblig> from s ;
    case oblig of
    S2x:S2(x);
    CFx:begin
        while not P(x) do
          begin
          S1(x);
          push <x,S2x> onto s;
          x := F(x)
          end;
        M(x)
        end { of case "CFx" }
    end { of cases on "oblig" }
  until s empty
  end { of procedure "C" };
```

In the second stage we note that only once is the obligation CFx pushed. We therefore replace the pushing of the obligation by the sequence for honouring it; and eliminate CFx as an obligation. We are left with a single obligation and so the notion can be eliminated entirely as shown in Fig. 8.15.

Fig. 8.15. The general linear schema derived from obligations.

```
procedure C(x:xtype);
  var s:stack of xtype;
  begin
  clear s;
  while not P(x) do
    begin
    S1(x);
    push x onto s;
    x := F(x)
    end;
  M(x);
  while s not empty do
```

```
          begin
          pop x from s;
          S2(x)
          end
        end { of procedure "C" };
```

It is, of course, precisely the same as that produced by the traditional technique used in the last section.

However the differences become more apparent when we consider other more general situations. Consider the general binary recursive schema of Fig. 8.16.

Fig. 8.16. A general binary recursive schema.
```
procedure C(x:xtype);
  begin
  if P(x) then M(x)
  else
    begin
    S1(x);
    C(F1(x));
    S2(x);
    C(F2(x));
    S3(x)
    end
  end { of procedure "C" };
```

A literal interpretation of the obligation technique produces the procedure of Fig. 8.17, provided that neither the statements $S1(x)$ and $S2(x)$, nor the evaluation of the parameters of calls $C(F1(x))$ and $C(F2(x))$ affects x.

Fig. 8.17. A literal version of the 'obligation' schema.
```
procedure C(x:xtype);
  type obligation = (CFx,S1x,S2x,S3x);
  var oblig:obligation;
      s:stack of <xtype,obligation>;
  begin
  clear s;
  push <x,CFx> onto s;
  repeat
    pop <x,oblig> from s;
    case oblig of
    S1x:S1(x);
    S2x:S2(x);
    S3x:S3(x);
    CFx:if P(x) then M(x)
        else
```

```
                  begin
                  push <x,S3x> onto s;
                  push <F2(x),CFx> onto s;
                  push <x,S2x> onto s;
                  push <F1(x),CFx> onto s;
                  push <x,S1x> onto s
                  end { of case "CFx" }
             end { of cases on "oblig" }
         until s empty
         end { of procedure "C" };
```

The restriction is due to the fact that the value of x used by $S1(x)$, $S2(x)$, $S3(x)$, $C(F1(x))$ and $C(F2(x))$ is stacked before any of those statements is obeyed. Once again we can improve this procedure using observations similar to those made earlier:

(i) There is no point pushing $\langle x, S1x \rangle$ onto s when we immediately pop it (on the next traverse of the loop) and perform $S1(x)$. We can instead just perform $S1(x)$.

(ii) This performance of $S1(x)$ can take place before the remaining pushes.

(iii) There is no point pushing $\langle F1(x), CFx \rangle$ onto s, and immediately popping it. The whole CFx obligation can be written as a loop.

The improved version is given in Fig. 8.18.

Fig. 8.18. A non-recursive binary schema based on obligations.

```
procedure C(x:xtype);
  type obligation = (CFx,S2x,S3x);
  var oblig:obligation;
      s:stack of <xtype,obligation>;
  begin
  clear s;
  push <x,CFx> onto s;
  repeat
    pop <x,oblig> from s;
    case oblig of
    S2x:S2(x);
    S3x:S3(x);
    CFx:begin
        while not P(x) do
          begin
          S1(x);
          push <x,S3x> onto s;
          push <F2(x),CFx> onto s;
          push <x,S2x> onto s;
          x := F1(x)
          end;
        M(x)
        end { of case "CFx" }
    end { of cases on "oblig" }
  until s empty
  end { of procedure "C" };
```

The restrictions on $S1(x)$ and $C(F1(x))$ no longer apply. Even so it is impossible to use this technique directly on Ackermann's procedure, because in the pair of calls:

$CalcAck(Ack,m,n{-}1)$

$CalcAck(Ack,m{-}1,Ack)$

the evaluation of the first produces a value Ack, which is a parameter of the second.

Simpler forms arise when we consider special cases. Fig. 8.19 gives the preorder case, which is (surprisingly?) simple.

Fig. 8.19. A non-recursive preorder schema based on obligations.

```
procedure C(x:xtype);
  var s:stack of xtype;
  begin
  clear s;
  push x onto s;
  repeat
    pop x from s;
    while not P(x) do
      begin
      S1(x);
      push F2(x) onto s;
      x := F1(x)
      end;
    M(x)
  until s empty
  end { of procedure "C" };
```

We encourage the reader to produce this schema from the general schema himself and to produce similar schemata for the inorder and postorder cases.

The advantages of this technique of direct use of the stack are that it is relatively simple to implement and that it produces a structured procedure immediately. Furthermore it is possible to think directly in the terms of the resulting procedure.

Its disadvantages are two-fold. Firstly, because all the obligations are stacked at once, it uses more store than the recursive version. Secondly, the technique is not completely general, because the resulting procedure causes expressions to be evaluated and statements to be obeyed out of order. Thus some procedures simply cannot be handled.

8.4 Body substitution

The third technique we will consider concentrates on the substantive statements obeyed by the recursive procedure, and seeks an iterative control structure to replace the recursive one. Let us return again to the general linear schema of Fig. 8.4, and consider what statements are obeyed when this procedure is called. Provided $P(x)$ is false, a call $C(x)$ will cause the three statements:

$$S1(x); \quad C(F(x)); \quad S2(x)$$

to be obeyed. Similarly if $P(F(x))$ is false, $C(F(x))$ will cause the three statements:

$$S1(F(x)); \quad C(F(F(x))); \quad S2(F(x))$$

to be obeyed. Let us adopt the shorthand of dropping all brackets and replacing a string of n $F's$ by F^n. Then if PF^nx is true (and PF^ix is false for all $i<n$) then the sequence of statements is:

$$S_1x$$
$$S_1Fx$$
$$S_1F^2x$$
$$\vdots$$
$$S_1F^{n-1}x$$
$$MF^nx$$
$$S_2F^{n-1}x$$
$$\vdots$$
$$S_2F^2x$$
$$S_2Fx$$
$$S_2x$$

Clearly we have two loops involved here. The first loop can be easily expressed:

> **while not** $P(x)$ **do**
> > **begin**
> > $S1(x);$
> > $x := F(x)$
> > **end**

The second loop requires the same values for x but in the reverse order. Thus the use of a stack to hold these values suggests itself and we arrive at the procedure of Fig. 8.20.

Fig. 8.20. The structured non-recursive schema.

```
procedure C(x:xtype);
  var s:stack of xtype;
  begin
  clear s;
  while not P(x) do
```

```
      begin
      S1(x);
      push x onto s;
      x := F(x)
      end;
   M(x);
   while s not empty do
      begin
      pop x from s;
      S2(x)
      end
   end { of procedure "C" };
```

It is, of course, the same schema as produced by the other two techniques.

It is when we move onto more general forms of recursion that the differences in the techniques manifest themselves, as we have already noticed. Consider again the general binary recursive schema reproduced as Fig. 8.21.

Fig. 8.21. A general binary recursive schema.
```
procedure C(x:xtype);
   begin
   if P(x) then M(x)
   else
      begin
      S1(x);
      C(F1(x));
      S2(x);
      C(F2(x));
      S3(x)
      end
   end { of procedure "C" };
```

To produce a non-recursive schema, we can proceed as before with the substitution process. Thus provided $P(x)$ is false, a call $C(x)$ will cause the five statements:

$$S1(x); \quad C(F1(x)); \quad S2(x); \quad C(F2(x)); \quad S3(x)$$

to be obeyed. Similarly, if $P(F1(x))$ is false, $C(F1(x))$ causes the five statements:

$$S1(F1(x)); \quad C(F1(F1(x))); \quad S2(F1(x));$$
$$C(F2(F1(x))); \quad S3(F1(x))$$

to be obeyed. If on the other hand $P(F1(x))$ is true then $C(F1(x))$ causes $M(F1(x))$ to be obeyed. A similar statement is true, independently, of $P(F2(x))$ and $C(F2(x))$.

Because of the binary nature of this schema the linear string produced by these substitutions is difficult to assimilate. A better display arises from using a tree representation as in Fig. 8.22 in which we have used the same abbreviating conventions as earlier. The three statements relevant to each activation are placed around the node in a way that suggests the order in which they are obeyed.

Fig. 8.22. The substitutions in the binary schema.

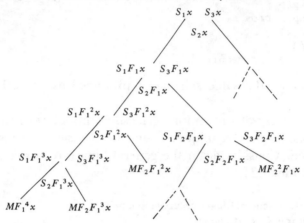

Using terminology appropriate to this tree of procedure calls, we see that each node is visited three times. We start at the root, and follow left branches, obeying an $S1$-statement at each node until we reach a leaf where we obey an M-statement. For the tree of Fig. 8.22 this will cause the sequence: S_1x, S_1F_1x, $S_1F_1^2x$, $S_1F_1^3x$, MF_1^4x to be obeyed. We then ascend to the node above, and, this being the second visit to the node, we obey an $S2$-statement. We then follow its right branch. In Fig. 8.22 this leads to a leaf and so we obey $MF_2F_1^3x$, though, in general, it would be an internal node so we would obey an $S1$-statement and descend down left branches to a leaf. To return to Fig. 8.22, after obeying $MF_2F_1^3x$ we ascend to the node above. As this is the third visit to the node we obey $S_3F_1^3x$ and ascend again. This is our second visit to this node and so we obey $S_2F_1^2x$ and descend.

Clearly we have alternating sequences of descent and ascent, the whole terminating after obeying $S3(x)$ at which point the stack will be empty. An appropriate schema is given in Fig. 8.23.

Fig. 8.23. A non-recursive binary schema.

```
procedure C(x:xtype);
   type statetype = (descent,ascent,done);
   var visit:2..3;
       state:statetype;
       s:stack of <xtype,2..3>;
```

```
begin
clear s;
state := descent;
repeat
  while not P(x) do
    begin
    S1(x);
    push <x,2> onto s;
    x := F1(x)
    end;
  M(x);
  state := ascent;
  repeat
    if empty(s) then state := done
    else
      begin
      pop <x,visit> from s;
      case visit of
      2: begin
        S2(x);
        push <x,3> onto s;
        x := F2(x);
        state := descent
        end { of case 2 };
      3: S3(x)
      end { of cases on "visit" }
      end
  until state <> ascent
until state = done
end { of procedure "C" };
```

This schema is, of course, very general and much simpler schemata can be produced for the special cases of preorder, inorder and post-order procedures. In Fig. 8.24 we give the preorder version, that is one in which $S2(x)$ and $S3(x)$ are both null. Note that we have to stack only x and the notion of a *statetype* disappears.

Fig. 8.24. A non-recursive preorder schema.

```
procedure C(x:xtype);
  var s:stack of xtype;
      done:Boolean;
  begin
  clear s;
  repeat
    while not P(x) do
      begin
      S1(x);
      push x onto s;
      x := F1(x)
      end;
```

```
        M(x);
        done := s empty;
        if not done then
          begin
          pop x from s;
          x := F2(x)
          end
      until done
      end { of procedure "C" };
```

This schema seems radically different from the general procedure from which it is derived – and yet it is a simplification of it. The reader is encouraged to take a copy of the procedure of Fig. 8.23 and systematically transform it by following through the consequences of making $S3(x)$ and $S2(x)$ null. It is easier to consider $S3(x)$ first.

He is also encouraged to produce similar schemata for the inorder and postorder procedures.

Note that this schema is quite different from the preorder schema of Fig. 8.19 which is based on obligations.

8.5   Parameters called as variables

None of the techniques we have discussed will deal with a parameter called as a variable. Thus we cannot transform the *CopyList* procedure of Fig. 2.3, which is reproduced as Fig. 8.25.

Fig. 8.25. A recursive version of *CopyList*.
```
procedure CopyList(var l1:listptr; l2:listptr);
  begin
  if l2 = nil then l1 := nil
  else
    begin
    new(l1);
    l1↑.item := l2↑.item;
    CopyList(l1↑.next,l2↑.next)
    end
  end { of procedure "CopyList" };
```

The reason for the prohibition is quite simple. If x consists only of value parameters we wish within the loop to replace x by $F(x)$ and the assignment $x := F(x)$ does it for us. Suppose now that x contains some parameter called as a variable, say v. Then v will be the name of some variable and within the loop we wish to change the variable of which it is the name. Unfortunately Pascal has no such facility. If it did (if for example $v = v1$ caused v to become the name of $v1$) we could simply produce the procedure of Fig. 8.26.

182

Fig. 8.26. An invalid non-recursive version of *CopyList*.

```
procedure CopyList(var l1:listptr; l2:listptr);
   begin
   while l2 <> nil do
      begin
      new(l1);
      l1↑.item := l2↑.item;
      l1 = l1↑.next;
      l2 := l2↑.next
      end;
   l1 := nil
   end { of procedure "CopyList" };
```

Such a solution is effectively available in Algol 68 but not in Pascal (see Bird (1979)). In Pascal we have to restructure the procedure so that the parameters in the recursive call are called by value. This implies a two-level solution. There are two techniques which lead to the two different forms of non-recursive procedure that we saw in Chapter 2. Both techniques transmit as the first parameter, not the name of the variable into which the copy will be placed, but the name of the node whose link points to the variable in which the copy will be placed. This is clearly the trailing pointer idea introduced in Chapter 2. In the first technique, the first node, if there is one, is dealt with separately, as shown in Fig. 8.27.

Fig. 8.27. A modified recursive version of *CopyList*.

```
procedure CopyList(var l1:listptr; l2:listptr);

   procedure C(p,l2:listptr);
      begin
      if l2 = nil then p↑.next := nil
      else
         begin
         new(p↑.next);
         p↑.next↑.item := l2↑.item;
         C(p↑.next,l2↑.next)
         end
      end { of procedure "C" };

   begin
   if l2 = nil then l1 := nil
   else
      begin
      new(l1);
      l1↑.item := l2↑.item;
      C(l1,l2↑.next)
      end
   end { of procedure "CopyList" };
```

The application of the preorder schema to this procedure produces the non-recursive one of Fig. 2.5.

With the second technique a node is created initially, the second list is produced with this acting as a header, and at the end this list is beheaded. The enclosed procedure *C* remains that of Fig. 8.27, and the body of *CopyList* becomes:

Fig. 8.28. An alternative body for *CopyList*.

```
begin
new(l1);
C(l1,l2);
Behead(l1)
end { of procedure "CopyList" };
```

Applying the preorder schema to this produces the version of Fig. 2.6.

These trailing pointer techniques need supplementing when applied to a tree since we need to know whether it is the left or right branch of the node in front of the trailing pointer that is involved, for which purpose we introduce a variable of type *branch* defined:

$$\textbf{type } branch = (l,r)$$

Consider the procedure *InsertOnTree* whose recursive version, given in Fig. 3.2, is reproduced as Fig. 8.29.

Fig. 8.29. A recursive version of *InsertOnTree*.

```
procedure InsertOnTree(var t:treeptr; it:itemtype);

  procedure I(var t:treeptr);
    begin
    if t = nil then NewTree(t,nil,it,nil)
    else if it.key = t↑.item.key then { item already there }
    else if it.key < t↑.item.key then I(t↑.left)
    else { if it.key > t↑.item.key then } I(t↑.right)
    end { of procedure "I" };

  begin
  I(t)
  end { of procedure "InsertOnTree" };
```

Rather than labour the point we simply give in Fig. 8.30 a procedure *InsertOnTree* in which *I* has only value parameters. We use the technique of adding a header and, for variety, use two pointers with $t2$ trailing $t1$. The statement *Behead(t)* stands for a sequence that beheads *t* that is known to have only a left branch, and *dummy* is a global variable.

184

Fig. 8.30. A recursive version of *InsertOnTree* with value parameters.

```
procedure InsertOnTree(var t:treeptr; it:itemtype);
  type branch = (l,r);

  procedure I(tl,t2:treeptr; b:branch);
    begin
    if tl = nil then
      if b = l then NewTree(t2↑.left,nil,it,nil)
      else NewTree(t2↑.right,nil,it,nil)
    else if it.key = tl↑.item.key then { item already there }
    else if it.key < tl↑.item.key then I(tl↑.left,tl,l)
    else { if it.key > tl↑.item.key then } I(tl↑.right,tl,r)
    end { of procedure "I" };

  begin
  NewTree(t,t,dummy,nil);
  I(t↑.left,t,l);
  Behead(t)
  end { of procedure "InsertOnTree" };
```

The reader can then produce an iterative solution very easily.

8.6   Some problems in conforming to the schema

It is generally trivial to convert most of the procedure of Chapter 1 into the form of the schema of Fig. 8.4. However, with the procedures of Chapters 2 and 3 there are two problems of interest which we consider in turn.

First, what Barron and Mullins (1978) have called the *protasis problem*. Consider the function *InList* of Fig. 2.7, with its inner function *I* expressed as a procedure, as shown in Fig. 8.31.

Fig. 8.31. The function *InList*.

```
function InList(l:listptr; k:keytype):Boolean;

  procedure I(l:listptr);
    begin
    if l = nil then InList := false
    else if k = l↑.item.key then InList := true
    else I(l↑.next)
    end { of procedure "I" };

  begin
  I(l)
  end { of function "InList" };
```

We cannot simply recast procedure *I* as shown in Fig. 8.32, because, when *l* = **nil**, *l*↑.*item* is undefined and hence the whole Boolean expression is undefined.

185

Fig. 8.32. An invalid version of *I*.

```
procedure I(1:listptr);
  begin
  if (1 = nil) or (k = 1↑.item.key) then
    InList := 1 <> nil
  else I(1↑.next)
  end { of procedure "I" };
```

However, we can ignore this problem for the moment and apply the appropriate schema, here the preorder one, to give a non-recursive procedure which is still invalid as shown in Fig. 8.33.

Fig. 8.33. An invalid non-recursive version of *I*.

```
procedure I(1:listptr);
  begin
  while (1 <> nil) and (k <> 1↑.item.key) do
    1 := 1↑.next;
  InList := 1 <> nil
  end { of procedure "I" };
```

This procedure can now be turned into valid Pascal by the classical technique of introducing a Boolean variable, which we will call *found*. If we then substitute the body of *I* for the call within *InList* we arrive at the non-recursive function of Fig. 8.34.

Fig. 8.34. The non-recursive function *InList*.

```
function InList(1:listptr; k:keytype):Boolean;
  var found:Boolean;
  begin
  found := false;
  while (1 <> nil) and not found do
    if k = 1↑.item.key then found := true
    else 1 := 1↑.next;
  InList := found
  end { of function "InList" };
```

Alternatively we can produce a version based on the notion of a state variable as shown in Fig. 8.35.

Fig. 8.35. A second non-recursive function *InList*.

```
function InList(1:listptr; k:keytype):Boolean;
  var state:(searching,notthere,found);
  begin
  state := searching;
  repeat
    if 1 = nil then state := notthere
    else if k = 1↑.item.key then state := found
    else 1 := 1↑.next
  until state <> searching;
  InList := state = found
  end { of function "InList" };
```

It is possible to produce a pair of equivalent schemata to match this class of procedure more directly but we leave this as an exercise to the reader.

A second problem in conforming to the schema arises where a procedure, such as *Power* from Chapter 1 and some tree processing procedures of Chapter 3, has a number of recursive calls only one of which is obeyed at each recursive level. One such is *OnTree* of Fig. 3.2 which is reproduced as Fig. 8.36. Note that it also exhibits the protasis problem.

Fig. 8.36. The recursive function *OnTree*.

```
function OnTree(t:treeptr; k:keytype):Boolean;

    procedure O(t:treeptr);
    begin
    if t = nil then Ontree := false
    else if k = t↑.item.key then OnTree := true
    else if k < t↑.item.key then O(t↑.left)
    else { if k > t↑.item.key then }  O(t↑.right)
    end { of procedure "O" };

    begin
    O(t)
    end { of function "OnTree" };
```

To conform to the general schema, the procedure *O* has to be recast so that there is only one recursive call. This requires the introduction of a local variable as shown in Fig. 8.37. Once again the resulting procedure is invalid because the Boolean expression is undefined.

Fig. 8.37. An invalid procedure *O*.

```
procedure O(t:treeptr);
    var local:treeptr;
    begin
    if (t = nil) or (k = t↑.item.key) then OnTree := t <> nil
    else
      begin
      if k < t↑.item.key then local := t↑.left
      else local := t↑.right;
      O(local)
      end
    end { of procedure "O" };
```

From here, using the preorder schema and the state variable technique of the last section, we can produce the non-recursive function of Fig. 8.38.

Fig. 8.38. A non-recursive function *OnTree*.

```
function OnTree(t:treeptr; k:keytype):Boolean;
  var state:(searching,notthere,found);
  begin
  state := searching;
  repeat
    if t = nil then state := notthere
    else if k = t↑.item.key then state := found
    else if k < t↑.item.key then t := t↑.left
    else t := t↑.right
  until state <> searching;
  OnTree := state = found
  end { of function "OnTree" };
```

Note that we have been able to eliminate *local*. Indeed, if Pascal had allowed conditional expressions, we need not have introduced it in the first place. We could have replaced the alternative sequence of Fig. 8.37 by:

$$O(\text{if } k < t\uparrow.item.key \text{ then } t\uparrow.left \text{ else } t\uparrow.right)$$

Thus if we were to create a system for doing this conversion automatically it might be convenient to expand Pascal to include conditional expressions (purely for internal operations of course).

EXERCISES

8.1 Consider the linear schema of Fig. 8.39.

Fig. 8.39. Another linear schema.

```
procedure C(x:xtype);
  begin
  S0(x);
  if P(x) then M(x)
  else
    begin
    S1(x);
    C(F(x));
    S2(x)
    end
  end { of procedure "C" };
```

Produce an equivalent non-recursive schema. What simplification arises if $S2(x)$ is null?

8.2 Consider the schema of Fig. 8.40, which might be appropriate to procedures that would run into the protasis problem if they were converted to the standard schema.

Fig. 8.40. Yet another linear schema.

```
procedure C(x:xtype);
  begin
  if P1(x) then M1(x)
  else if P2(x) then M2(x)
  else
    begin
    S1(x);
    C(F(x));
    S2(x)
    end
  end { of procedure "C" };
```

Produce an equivalent non-recursive schema.

Further reading and references

Much of the material of this book comes from the folklore of computer science, and it is very difficult to attribute the techniques to any specific author. What we can do is mention a number of books in which different examples are presented or in which a different view is propounded.

Two important books which use Pascal as a vehicle are Wirth's *Algorithms + Data Structures = Programs* and Alagic and Arbib's *The Design of Well-Structured and Correct Programs*. A number of examples used here derive from them.

As we have seen, recursive procedures arise naturally in relation to recursive data structures and many of the more recent texts on that subject use recursion with facility. One such is *Data Structures using Pascal* by Tenenbaum and Augenstein.

These books are practical books about programming in Pascal and are quite easy to read. There are three books in particular which are rather more abstract and correspondingly more difficult to read. These are Burge's *Recursive Programming Techniques*, Bauer and Wossner's *Algorithmic Language and Program Development*, and Wand's *Induction, Recursion and Programming*.

We noted in the preface that recursion is the predominant control structure in functional programming. The reader whose appetite has been whetted by this book might like to look at this aspect. An excellent modern text is Henderson's *Functional Programming: Application and Implementation*.

One area where we can attribute techniques to workers is the elimination of recursion, since this is a current area of research. In the bibliography below we include what seems to us to be the most important papers, by Darlington & Burstall, Bird, Arsac and Rohl. These should act as a good starting point for a search of the literature.

Further reading

Alagic, S. & Arbib, M. A., *The Design of Well-Structured and Correct Programs*, Springer-Verlag, 1978.
Arsac, J., 'Syntactic source to source transforms and program manipulation', *Comm. ACM*, pp. 43–53 (1979).

Bauer, F. L. & Wossner, H., *Algorithmic Language and Program Development*, Springer-Verlag, 1982.

Bird, R. S., 'Notes on recursion elimination', *Comm. ACM.* Vol. 20, pp. 434-9, (1977).

Burge, W. H., *Recursive Programming Techniques*, Addison-Wesley, 1975.

Darlington, J. & Burstall, R. M., 'A system which automatically improves programs', *Proc. 3rd. Int. Conf. on Artificial Intelligence*, Stanford University, pp. 479-85 (1973).

Henderson, P., *Functional Programming: Application and Implementation*, Prentice-Hall, 1980.

Rohl, J. S., 'Eliminating recursion from combinational procedures', *Software Practice & Experience*, Vol. 11, pp. 803-17 (1981).

Tenenbaum, A. M. & Augenstein, M. J., *Data Structures using Pascal*, Prentice-Hall, 1981.

Wand, M., *Induction, Recursion and Programming*, Elsevier, North Holland, 1980.

Wirth, N., *Algorithms + Data Structures = Programs*, Prentice-Hall, 1976.

References

Atkinson, L. V., 'Know the state you are in', *Pascal News*, No. 13, p. 66 (1978).

Barron, D. W., *Recursive Techniques in Programming*, MacDonald, 1968.

Barron, D. W. & Mullins, J. M., 'What to do after a **while**', *Pascal News*, 11 (1978).

Bird, R. S., 'Recursion elimination with variable parameters', *Comp. J.*, Vol 22, pp. 151-4 (1979).

Knuth, D. E., *The Art of Computer Programming*, Vol. 3, Addison-Wesley, 1973.

Knuth, D. E., 'Structured programming with goto statements, *Computing Surveys* Vol. 6, pp. 261-302 (1974).

Knuth, D. E. & Merner, J. N., 'Algol 60 confidential', *Comm. ACM*, Vol 4, pp. 208-72 (1961).

Goldschlager, L. M., 'Short algorithms for space-filling curves', *Software Practice & Experience*, Vol. 11, p. 99 (1981).

Leuker, G. S., 'Some techniques for solving recurrences', *Computing Surveys*, Vol. 12, pp. 419-36 (1980).

Rohl, J. S. & Barrett, H. J., *Programming via Pascal*, Cambridge University Press, 1980.

Rohl, J. S. & Gedeon, T. D., 'Four Tower Hanoi and beyond', *Australian Computer Science Comm.*, Vol. 5, p. 156 (1983).

Sedgewick, R. 'Permutation generation methods', *Computing Surveys*, Vol. 9, pp. 137-164 (1977).

Zahn, C. T., 'A control statement for natural top-down structured programming', presented at the Symposium on Programming Languages, Paris, 1974.

191

Index of procedures

This index contains the numbers of all the figures relevant to a given procedure. Only free-standing procedures are given in this index: internal procedures are referenced under the name of the procedures they are to be embedded in.